ANNEMARIE VELS HEIJN
REMBRANDT

THE LITTLE ART BOOK
In English, French, German, Spanish,
Dutch and Italian editions
Edited by BERTHOLD FRICKE

ANNEMARIE VELS HEIJN

Rembrandt

With 60 Colour Illustrations
from the works of the master, his teachers,
pupils, friends and contemporaries

Translated from the Dutch
by W. Keith Haughan

KNORR & HIRTH VERLAG GMBH
D-3167 AHRBECK/HANNOVER

Photos:

André Held, Ecublens (Vd) 1

Knorr & Hirth, Ahrbeck 2, 9, 12, 16, 28, 29, 30, 33, 38, 40, 46, 49, 58, 60

Rijksmuseum, Amsterdam 3, 4, 5, 6, 7, 8, 10, 17, 18, 19, 20, 22, 23, 24, 25, 27, 31, 32, 36, 37, 42, 43, 44, 47, 48, 50, 51, 52, 56, 57

National Gallery, London 11, 21, 53

Mauritshuis, Den Haag 13

Staatliche Kunstsammlungen, Kassel 14, 35, 45

Städelsches Kunstinstitut, Frankfurt 15

Museum Boymans-Van Beuningen, Rotterdam 26, 41

Collectie Jan Six, Amsterdam 34

Giraudon, Paris 39

Nationalmuseum, Stockholm 54

Herzog Anton Ulrich-Museum, Braunschweig 55

M. H. de Young Memorial Museum, San Francisco 59

©
Knorr & Hirth Verlag GmbH
1973 / 1977 / 1981
Printed in West Germany
ISBN 3-7821-2500-2

REMBRANDT AND HIS WORLD

A good painter is not always good at teaching people how to paint as well. Rembrandt was a good painter — his paintings prove that. It is not known whether Rembrandt was also a good master, unless one claims that quality gives its own proof. Then, the fact that it is known of thirty-five painters that they were pupils of Rembrandt's is a proof of Rembrandt's quality as a master. That he did, in reality, have many more pupils is indeed most probable.

In the seventeenth century, painting was not a matter of inspiration, of waiting for a whisper from Lady Inspiration. A seventeenth-century painter was a tradesman, who painted just as another man baked bread or made cupboards. And for such a trade, an apprenticeship was necessary. The guilds had all made definite rules about that. The painters' guild, St. Luke's, had stipulated that a painter had to be a pupil for the length of three years before he could call himself a master. In these three years, the work done by the pupil was the property of the master. He could sell it under his own name. Only after his period of training could a painter sign his own work himself, or sell it under his own name, and then he was also bound to pay contributions to the guild.

The painter's training naturally consisted of many technical parts: mixing paint (painters made their own paint in the seventeenth century), filling wooden panels and canvases, drawing models, from plaster casts or from a living model.

Arnold Houbraken recounts in his *Great Survey of Artists and Paintings* that Rembrandt had so many pupils in the '30s that he rented a warehouse on the Bloemgracht, in order to accommodate the pupils. A little room was partitioned off there for each pupil with paper and sailcloth, and there each of them could work quietly by himself with a live model.

Every now and then, the master would go round to supervise and improve the work of the pupils. Later, when Rembrandt had his own house on the Anthoniesbreestraat, he had little rooms made in the attic there.

The notion of 'plagiarism' — one of the worst reproaches one can make to an artist nowadays — did not exist in the seventeenth century. It was quite common to use others' good finds in one's own work.

A pupil could therefore copy not only the work of his master (and also a master the work of his pupil of course), but also compositions of other artists, mostly known from engravings — a part of every proper studio inventory — which were copied and eventually worked into his own productions.

Pupils were usually boarded with their master. They paid about 100 guilders a year for bed, board and laundry; and naturally their training was included in this.

How Rembrandt imparted this training to his pupils is not known; there is really nothing known about Rembrandt and his pupils, apart from what can finally be gathered from the work of master and pupils. It is very likely that Rembrandt sold his pupils' work under his own name — that was the officially allowed custom. It is not really possible now to make out the work from Rembrandt's own hand.

Yet we can hardly distinguish more surely the influence of the master in the work that Rembrandt's pupils did after their period of training. A good master must never impose his own style on his pupils. As regards that, Rembrandt must indeed deserve the name of a good master: he allowed his pupils to develop the facets of their personality entirely in their own way.

Stephen was one of the seven preachers whom Jesus' disciples had appointed among the Greeks. In the Acts of the Apostles, it is stated that he "was full of grace and strength" and "performed miracles and great deeds among the people." But that aroused jealousy. His enemies led him "before the Council". Stephen's testimony there moved them to rage, for he appealed to their conscience. "They began to shout at the top of their voices, stopped up their ears and stormed at him all together; and they threw him out of the city and stoned him."

This painting was discovered in the store-room of the museum at Lyon in 1962: when it was cleaned, it was seen to be signed by Rembrandt and dated 1625. It is thus the earliest known painting by him up to the present time.

Rembrandt had then only just finished his apprenticeship. At first, he had been apprenticed to Jacob van Swanenburgh in Leiden and then later, for half a year in 1624, to Pieter Lastman in Amsterdam. Rembrandt did not want to go to Italy, although it was thought that a painter's training was not really complete if he had not sojourned for a time in Rome. There are enough Italian paintings in Holland, as he said to Constantijn Huygens, when the latter was paying a visit to Rembrandt's workshop. By this, Rembrandt also meant perhaps the paintings 'in the Italian manner' which painters like his teacher Pieter Lastman, who had once been in Italy, executed when they were back at home. Rembrandt wished to imitate this kind of painting in his "Stoning of St. Stephen". The figures are still a little stiffly executed, and the whole, or all the parts of the painting somewhat clumsily put together: the darker figures on the left, the group of stoners with Stephen in his priest's garments as the focal point, and in the background, on a hill, Saul, with the clothes of the stoners on his lap.

That Rembrandt has put Saul in such a prominent position is not strange. Saul, who, as Paul, became the greatest fighter for Christendom after his conversion, was a character who fascinated Rembrandt. That Saul, as the Bible recounts, was a witness to the stoning of Stephen and had even held the clothes of the stoners there, was given some significance by Rembrandt in his painting.

1. REMBRANDT VAN RIJN
Born 15th July 1606 at Leiden
Died 4th October 1669 in Amsterdam

THE STONING OF ST. STEPHEN
Wood, 89.5 cms. × 123.6 cms.
signed and dated: 1625:
Lyon, Musée des Beaux Arts.

Rembrandt was naturally not the only artist who has ever depicted the story of the stoning of St. Stephen. Many artists before him had attempted the same subject.

Three years after Rembrandt's 'Stoning of St. Stephen' (plate 1) was discovered in Lyon, this painting by Adam Elsheimer was found — in 1965 — in a house in Edinburgh. And then it transpired that it was very probable that Rembrandt knew Elsheimer's 'Stoning' when he painted his own 'Stoning of St. Stephen'. But Rembrandt could certainly not have seen Elsheimer's picture in the original. Adam Elsheimer was a foreigner. But he worked in Italy for practically the whole of his life, at first in Venice and later, from 1600, in Rome. It was in Rome that Elsheimer executed this picture. Many foreigners were living in Rome at the time, and one of them was Sir Peter Paul Rubens. This Fleming made a drawing of Elsheimer's picture and, back in Antwerp, he had his pupil Peter Soutman make an engraving from it: thus, all who were interested could be acquainted with Elsheimer's picture. That was the way in which well-informed artists saw the productions of their colleagues abroad. In the inventory of every studio of that time there should be a portfolio with engravings of all kinds of works of art.

But in this case, Rembrandt had another source of information: his teacher Pieter Lastman had known Elsheimer well in Rome, at the very time when Elsheimer was working on the 'Stoning of St. Stephen'. Adam Elsheimer considered himself an Italian painter, though his Italian colleagues must have thought him extremely un-Italian. Everything that was fashionable in Italian art, Elsheimer used in his pictures: nude figures, carefully executed from an anatomical point of view, a host of angels coming elegantly from heaven fly down to bring the victor's wreath to Stephen, a landscape with a lot of trees and decorative ruins in the background, a number of colourfully-dressed spectators. From an engraving, Rembrandt was only informed concerning the form of Elsheimer's painting, but not at all about the colouring. From Elsheimer's original, Rembrandt created something that pleased the more sober Dutch painter.

2. ADAM ELSHEIMER
Baptised 18th March 1578 at Frankfurt-on-Main
Buried 11th December 1610 at Rome.

THE STONING OF ST. STEPHEN
Silvered copper, 34.5 cm. × 28.5 cm.
c. 1602–1605.
Edinburgh, National Gallery of Scotland.

Pieter Lastman was born in Amsterdam and had his training as a painter there. And, as behoved all progressive painters of the time around 1600, he went to Italy to round off his artistic training there. After his return to Amsterdam in 1607, he continued to turn out paintings full of memories of what he had learnt and seen in Italy. Naturally he also tried to impart his admiration for Italian art to his pupils. He should be very thankful to one of the pupils, Rembrandt, that due to the fact that he was his master, Lastman has a much more enduring place in Dutch painting than he would have deserved to have through his own efforts. A good pupil makes a teacher!

Artists who painted pictures inspired by Italian originals were eager to depict scenes from mythology. This is a scene from the adventures of Orestes, the son of Agamemnon, the king of Mycenæ. Orestes is instructed by the oracle at Delphi to go and fetch from Tauris an old image of Artemis, the goddess of hunting. He sets off, together with his bosom-friend Pylades, the son of the king of Phocis. But the young men are caught in the act of stealing, and one of them has to be sacrificed to the gods. The sacrificial ceremony is well under way, each of the friends wants to have himself sacrificed instead of the other. Then Iphigenia, the priestess in Tauris, discovers that one of the young men whom she has to sacrifice is her brother Orestes. She is able, by her cunning, to avert the sacrifice.

That Lastman learnt a lot from Elsheimer in Rome is very clear: Lastman is also colourful and fussy; everything is conscientiously rendered: the flowers, the fabrics, the parts of the procession with the — almost stolen — image of Artemis as its main trophy.

Rembrandt could not learn from his master how to depict more realistic deeds: Lastman's figures stand rigidly glued to the spot, and that should only be the fact with Iphigenia, who notices to her perplexity that her brother Orestes is the sacrificial victim.

3. PIETER LASTMAN
Born 1583 at Amsterdam
Buried 4th April 1633 at Amsterdam.

ORESTES AND PYLADES IN TAURIS
Wood, 83 cm. × 126 cm.
signed and dated: 1614;
Amsterdam, Rijksmuseum.

Tobit was a true servant of the God of Israel, even in defiance of the rulers of Israel. Even when he became blind through following the law of Moses, and could no longer do his work from then on, and was shut up in his house, he remained a faithful servant of God. Then his wife Anna earned scanty wages with her spinning. One day she came home with a kid which she had received as a present from one of her employers. Tobit heard the kid bleating and began to rail against Anna: he thought that she had stolen it. But then Anna was also angry: although he might be a true servant of God, he has now suspected his own wife of theft. Then Tobit is horrified by his own mistrust, and he prays to God to forgive him his unworthy behaviour. Anna, somewhat bewildered, looks on.

Rembrandt had a model when painting this picture: an engraving of a drawing by Willem Buytewech. In that work, the room, the objects in the room, and the figures seem similar to those in Rembrandt's painting. However, in Buytewech's drawing, Anna is just in the process of telling her husband the truth. Rembrandt chooses another moment, a moment with much more tension: Tobit's repentant prayer. Rembrandt may have been just beginning as a painter then; but he knew that it is not only good execution that makes a good painter and also, rightly, that the choice of subject and its content is very important. Both now and later, he quite often chose in biblical stories the moment in which there is contact between man and God, at times when men have to react to events, the intervention of God in their lives. And then Rembrandt also only filled the remaining space in the little painting in question with a very few objects: onions, the little birdcage, the little fire. He only found it necessary to include a bobbin to tell us that Anna earned her living by spinning. Later, even that much would distract the attention: men, the reactions of men were things which Rembrandt was always to think more important.

4. REMBRANDT VAN RIJN
Born 15th July 1606 at Leiden
Died 4th October 1669 at Amsterdam.

TOBIT AND ANNA WITH THE KID
Wood, 39.5 cm. × 30 cm.
signed and dated: 1626;
Amsterdam, Rijksmuseum,
on loan from Baroness Bentinck.

Rembrandt must have been in the region of his twenty-third year when he painted this portrait of himself. Yet it is really not a true portrait. It is a study of a laughing face, of his own face. This fascinated Rembrandt greatly in his first years as a painter: the movements of a face, in astonishment, in joy, in grief. And in paintings, drawings and etchings it was again and again his own face that he used for these studies. He always depicted the face so that it seems to be looking in a mirror: very direct and close to. A nose is therefore broader than it was in reality, as it was closer to the mirror.

Artists have, indeed, painted many self-portraits. In the seventeenth century, they posed eagerly and in a seemly fashion, as a respectable member of society; but only Rembrandt used such a strange selection of finery.

At this time, he was not yet calling himself Rembrandt. On the paintings he did in Leiden, he signed himself as RH (Rembrandt Harmenszoon), or as RHL (Rembrandt Harmenszoon of Leiden). Later, in Amsterdam, he would use his forename Rembrandt in full, but he really never used 'Van Rijn'.

His father had acquired the patronymic because the malt-mill which he owned at Leiden was called 'De Rijn'. Not really a very original name for a mill which stands on a place which was at one time the bank of the (Old) Rhine.

In this self-portrait, Rembrandt uses shades of brown and gold, colours which were to remain his favourites for the rest of his life. So many shades of brown are used in the background, that it is not a flat colour, but is as alive as every other part of the painting.

5. REMBRANDT VAN RIJN
Born 15th July 1606 at Leiden
Died 4th October 1669 at Amsterdam.

SELF-PORTRAIT
Wood, 41.5 cm. × 34 cm.
signed, c. 1629;
Amsterdam, Rijksmuseum.

Jeremiah was called to be a prophet in the thirteenth year of the reign of King Joshua (627 B. C.). In a divine vision, he was given the instruction "to cast down peoples and kingdoms in the name of the Lord". Jeremiah himself proclaimed that the invincible city of Jerusalem would be laid waste. In 586, he was proved right: the Babylonian king Nebuchadnezzar II destroyed Jerusalem; his army burnt down the royal palace, the Temple of Solomon and the dwellings of the prominent citizens. All the treasure from the temple was taken away as booty: dishes, plate and candelabra of gold and silver. Jeremiah wished to stay in Israel with the poor people whom the army left behind; the rest were taken away into exile at Babel.

In Rembrandt's painting, Jeremiah is seeing in a vision the horrors which are to overtake Jerusalem; God is showing him that only a true conversion of the people can save them from such a disaster. But no-one listens to Jeremiah's prediction.

Rembrandt very carefully depicted his Jeremiah as an old man. Earlier, in Leiden, Rembrandt made many drawings of old men; from such drawings as these the figure of Jeremiah could have been created.

Rembrandt gave the Jerusalem in the background the appearance which he imagined the city to have; he probably knew the printed pictures of Jerusalem which were in circulation in the seventeenth century. There too stands the round building which Rembrandt and many of his contemporaries took to be the temple. But this was really the Mosque of the Rock which the Arabs had built on the site of the Temple of Solomon in 691.

Religious pictures were hardly ever painted for the church in Protestant Holland, but for private individuals. This explains why they are so often small in format: they had to be made to hang in ordinary houses. Then no exalted saints were depicted either, but ordinary people who felt themselves to be addressed by the word of God.

6. REMBRANDT VAN RIJN
Born 15th July 1606 at Leiden
Died 4th October 1669 at Amsterdam.

THE PROPHET JEREMIAH
FORESEES THE DESTRUCTION
OF JERUSALEM
Wood, 58 cm. × 46 cm.
signed and dated: 1630;
Amsterdam, Rijksmuseum.

When Joseph and Mary brought their son Jesus to the Temple in Jerusalem "to present him to the Lord" and to sacrifice a pair of turtle-doves, the old prophetess Hannah was also in the Temple. She recognized in little Jesus the Messiah of whom the prophets had spoken so eagerly. Hannah was then 84 years old, says the Bible. She knew the Bible well, did Hannah, and for that reason Rembrandt also put a Bible in her hands; and the Hebrew characters in it can still be deciphered. And he also did his best to dress her in the fashion in which he imagined that an oriental prophetess would have appeared. It has often been supposed that Rembrandt's mother was the model for the prophetess.

Cornelia Willensdochter van Zuytbroeck, known as Neeltje, the mother of Rembrandt, married Harmen van Rijn in 1589. In 1631, she would have been a good sixty years old. We do not know what she looked like. Whether she really is the old woman whom Rembrandt depicted in countless paintings, drawings and etchings cannot be ascertained conclusively: Rembrandt never wrote on the back of any drawing or etching that the picture was of his mother.

It was in the year that Rembrandt painted this picture that he moved to Amsterdam for good. There he quickly gave up the painstaking fashion of painting on small-sized panels for larger canvases and wooden panels. As he painted a lot more loosely and rapidly, he became all the closer to the existing tradition in Amsterdam.

7. REMBRANDT VAN RIJN
Born 15th July 1606 at Leiden
Died 4th October 1669 at Amsterdam.

THE PROPHETESS HANNAH
"REMBRANDT'S MOTHER"
Wood, 60 cm. × 48 cm.
signed and dated: 1631;
Amsterdam, Rijksmuseum.

In 1628, Gerard Dou came as a pupil to "the skilled artist, the widely-celebrated master Rembrandt". Rembrandt was then twenty-two and Dou fifteen. Gerard Dou knew all about painting and was himself a member of the glaziers' guild in Leiden. The young man remained Rembrandt's pupil till 1631, when the master moved to Amsterdam. Rembrandt had a great influence on Gerard Dou, and when Rembrandt was using a completely different style of painting in Amsterdam, Dou was still painting on very finely-worked small wooden panels. His pupils and successors were themselves to use this method right into the eighteenth century.

Working together in the same studio, Rembrandt and Dou often painted the same models too. The old woman of this painting by Dou is probably the same one who also sat as a model for Rembrandt's prophetess Hannah (plate 7); she is propably not Rembrandt's mother either.

The book that the old woman is holding is not a Bible but a book of pericopes. In it are biblical texts for every Sunday, printed in full, and in addition to these, a woodcut that illustrates the gospel story. The books were given out by the Catholic Church: the Protestants used one or other of the Luther translations of the Bible for the most part, and there were no illustrations in these.

The old woman has the book of pericopes open at the 19th chapter of St. Luke: the story of Zacchaeus. Zacchaeus was the rich chief of the publicans (tax-inspectors) in Jericho. When Jesus came to visit Jericho, Zacchaeus climbed a fig-tree, in order to see Jesus that much better. Jesus stopped right by the fig-tree and said, "Come down here, Zacchaeus, for I want to come and eat at your house." After that, Zacchaeus was converted from his wicked ways as a tax-inspector.

In the seventeenth century, quite a lot of people, particularly women, could not read. Hence Dou does not have his old woman reading the text, but looking at the picture in the book. And it is very characteristic of Dou's precision: in the painting we can even see what the woodcut represents: Zacchaeus in the fig-tree, with Jesus and a disciple beneath.

8. GERARD DOU
Born 7th April 1613 at Leiden
Buried 9th February 1675 at Leiden.

AN OLD WOMAN
WITH A BOOK OF PERICOPES
"REMBRANDT'S MOTHER"
Wood, 71 cm. × 55.5 cm.
c. 1631;
Amsterdam, Rijksmuseum.

From the descriptions in the Bible, Rembrandt had grasped that the Temple of Solomon was incredibly beautiful. In a room of just such an unearthly beauty, rather like a gothic church, Rembrandt makes the Presentation in the Temple take place.

Joseph and Mary had to travel for three days in order to be able to present their son to the Lord in the Temple at Jerusalem. Simeon was also in the Temple. God had promised him that he would not die before he had seen the Lord's Messiah. And when Joseph and Mary came in with their son, Simeon recognized in Jesus the Messiah. He took the child in his arms and sang a hymn of praise to God.

No one in the Temple grasps what is really going on: some look on amazed, others pass through in their accustomed fashion. Their eyes seem closed to the golden stream of light which falls on the group at the foot of the stairs which lead to the throne of the High Priest. Mary has her arms crossed over her breast; she is, after the tradition in art, dressed in blue. Joseph is kneeling next to her; he is much younger than he is in most paintings. He has in his hands the sacrifice that they have just brought for the High Priest: two turtle-doves.

Usually Rembrandt has the viewer of his pictures standing directly in front of the scene. Here he is rather at a distance, because of the flagstones between the group round the Child and the spectator.

In the eighteenth century, it was the fashion to round off the upper part of paintings. With this painting by Rembrandt we also find the top two corners rounded off: as was usual for him, Rembrandt had painted it on a rectangular panel.

9. REMBRANDT VAN RIJN
Born 15th July 1606 at Leiden
Died 4th October 1669 at Amsterdam.

THE PRESENTATION IN THE TEMPLE
Wood, 61 cm. × 48 cm.
signed and dated: 1631;
The Hague, Mauritshuis.

Constantijn Huygens was an important figure in the cultural life of the Republic of the United Low Countries. As Secretary of the Council of State, following a period serving the Stadhouders Frederik Hendrik, Willem II and Willem III, he also had great influence in the field of art. He was himself very much interested in the arts: he wrote music, played several musical instruments himself and was a good poet.

It was probably in 1629 that Huygens and his brother Maurits paid a visit to Rembrandt's studio in Leiden, where Jan Lievens was also working. That visit could very well have been an exciting event for the two young painters. Huygens was much impressed by their work. In his autobiography he writes that the pair shall shortly surpass the artists whom Huygens had earlier named as a wonderful kind of people among mortals. Huygens also expatiates at great length about a portrait that Lievens had painted of him, not as a commission, but because the painter himself wanted to do it so much. He writes that some people think that he is depicted rather gloomily in state, but that is itself very good, thinks Huygens himself, as he sat at a time when he had indeed a great many worries.

Lievens painted Huygens' clothes and hands in the winter, and in spring he came back to it and completed the head. Huygens was very pleased with the picture.

The contact with Huygens was not unprofitable for Rembrandt and Lievens: Rembrandt obtained through Huygens the commission for the painting of a series of pictures of events from the Passion of Jesus for the Stadhouder Frederek Hendrik; thanks to Huygens' mediation, Lievens was able to make a journey to England in 1632.

As was Rembrandt, Lievens was in Amsterdam for half a year, to finish off his painter's education in Pieter Lastman's studio there. Once back in Leiden, the two young men seemed to be close friends.

In any case, in Huygen's opinion, Lievens was at the time the more promising of the two. But things fell out differently: Rembrandt made a great career in Amsterdam, Lievens could not find his niche in either England, Antwerp or Amsterdam.

10. JAN LIEVENS
Born 24th October 1607 at Leiden
Died 8th June 1674 at Amsterdam.

CONSTANTIJN HUYGENS (1596 - 1687),
SECRETARY TO THE
COUNCIL OF STATE
Wood, 99 cm. × 84 cm.
Amsterdam, Rijksmuseum,
on loan from the Musée
de la Chartreuse, Douai.

It was not really unusual for an important man like Constantijn Huygens to have his portrait painted. In the early 1620s, Thomas de Keyser was *the* portrait painter in Amsterdam and it is therefore hardly surprising that the connoisseur Huygens should have his portrait painted by this painter in 1627. Huygens held an important position in the political life in Holland, and so de Keyser depicted his commissioner in his study: as well as the bagfuls of letters which are lying unopened on the table, yet another arrives and is being brought in by a servant. But De Keyser, after the fashion of the time, also assembled symbols of Huygen's duties in the picture: on the chimney-breast, a painting of a ship, as a symbol of the ship of state; the orrery and globe as symbols of Huygen's universal knowledge; a lute, not just an indication of Huygen's interest in music, but symbolizing at the same time a quality needed in a good statesman: the ability to create harmony and accord from all opposing opinions and conceptions.

Thomas de Keyser could hardly have been very pleased that a young painter from Leiden, Rembrandt, obtained so many commissions for portraits from Amsterdam that he finally thought it more advisable to settle in this town in 1631. Rembrandt van Rijn did indeed seem a concurrent for Thomas de Keyser. Beside Rembrandt's much more lively style of portraiture, de Keyser's portraits soon seemed a little old-fashioned.

11. THOMAS DE KEYSER
Born 1596 or 1597 in Amsterdam
Buried 7th June 1667 in Amsterdam.

CONSTANTIJN HUYGENS (1596 - 1687),
SECRETARY TO THE
COUNCIL OF STATE,
AND HIS (?) CLERK
Wood, 92 cm. × 69 cm.
signed and dated: 1627;
London, National Gallery.

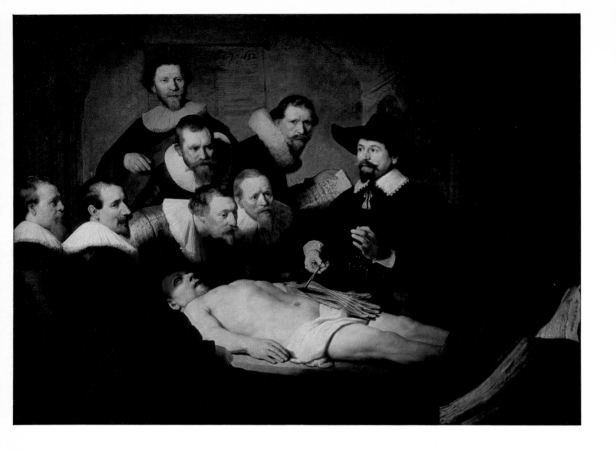

Just a little while after he became resident in Amsterdam, Rembrandt obtained, in 1632, a very important commission from the Surgeons' Guild of Amsterdam: the Anatomy Lesson of Dr. Nicolaes Tulp. Anatomy lessons were strange events: on only one occasion a year could incisions be made in the corpse of a person who had been condemned to death. Each lesson was accurately recorded in the Anatomy Book of the Surgeons' Guild, usually with the name of the victim and his offence beside it. Only in 1628 was a chair of anatomy inaugurated at Amsterdam, and the first to be the pre-elect in anatomy was Dr. Nicolaes Tulp. In January 1632, Dr. Tulp gave a public lesson on the physiology of the arm. The names of those who observed are known, as everyone can see them written down in the sketch-book that the man next to Dr. Tulp is holding in his hand, in that book where there seems at first to be only an anatomical drawing.

Rembrandt may well have been present at the lesson, but the painting was naturally composed later from separate portraits; Rembrandt probably copied the anatomy of the arm from the textbooks of anatomy that were available.

So many painters before Rembrandt had attempted to depict groups of people that Rembrandt must have been well aware of the problems that were involved in this. The master attempted to make a less stiff group by not positioning them close round the surgeon, and by making them look up at him all together from the other side. Dr. Tulp is speaking: he is making a gesture which has indicated speech in representational art since antiquity.

Rembrandt's painting came to hang in the anatomical theatre in the Weighing House in the Nieuwmarkt. Twenty-four years later, another Anatomy Lesson by Rembrandt was to be hung there: that of Dr. Deyman, the successor of Dr. Tulp as lecturer in anatomy (plate 43).

12. REMBRANDT VAN RIJN
Born 15th July 1606 at Leiden
Died 4th October 1669 at Amsterdam.

THE ANATOMY LESSON
OF DR. NICOLAES TULP
Canvas, 162.5 cm. × 216.5 cm.
signed and dated: 1632;
The Hague, Mauritshuis.

In the seventeenth century, children were really nothing more than small grown-ups, and from their twelfth year onwards, they were gradually considered more and more as adults. They learnt to read and write early; the examples of young people who had completed their academic studies before they were twenty were legion — and they were not really the prodigies of their age. In the opinion of the people living in the seventeenth century, there were no subjects at all which were "for grown-ups only"; a child was just a different, younger person, and the idea that these different people were not 'ripe' for certain things did not exist at that time.

The boy in the portrait by Jacob Backer is, completely in accordance with these ideas, just such a young adult; apart from the fact that his suit is smaller than a gentleman's costume, there is not a single difference.

Protestant Dutchmen favoured subdued colours for clothing. For a painter, it was therefore not so simple to make such a soberly-clad man or woman into a living portrait. That is why Backer did not omit from the picture the little red cord with which the white collar was fastened so tightly.

Jacob Backer was born in Harlingen (Friesland) and he went to Leeuwarden, not far from there, to be a painter. In this town he met Govert Flinck, and the young painters went on together to the then distant Amsterdam. There, Backer and Flinck very quickly became acquainted with Rembrandt. It seems that they had heard of his existence in Leeuwarden.

Govert Flinck became a pupil of Rembrandt's. Backer was far too old to be able to become a painter's pupil, but the influence of the master asserted itself in his work: this portrait was itself thought to be a Rembrandt for a time.

13. Jacob Backer
Born 1608 at Harlingen
Died 27th August 1651 at Amsterdam.

Portrait of a Boy
"The Boy in Grey"
Canvas, 94 cm. × 71 cm.
signed and dated: 1634;
The Hague, Mauritshuis.

On 22nd June 1634, Rembrandt married Saskia van Uylenburgh in the Reformed Church in the parish of Sint Anna in Friesland. A year earlier, on the occasion of their engagement, he had made a drawing of her on prepared paper with a silver pencil. He had written underneath the drawing: *this is a drawing of my wife who was 21 years old on the bord day after we were married* (= engaged), *on 8th June 1633*. And thus we know what Saskia looked like.

If one follows this little portrait the likeness of Saskia seems to appear in many of Rembrandt's portraits and paintings with young women. Whether or not this controversy is not quickly to determine. This young woman with red hair really is somewhat like Saskia. The carnation which this vaguely familiar woman is holding in her right hand is sometimes seen in other portraits, and is probably just a symbol of marriage; perhaps this is therefore a portrait on the occasion of Rembrandt's own marriage. But perhaps it is just a portrait of an attractive woman, which Rembrandt painted for no particular reason, for his own pleasure; it could also be a commissioned work, and it is not impossible that he was here depicting a certain historical personage whom we no longer recognize now. It is unlikely that any Dutch woman really wore the fantastic costume.

To the consternation of Constantijn Huygens, who writes about it in his autobiography, Rembrandt did not find it necessary to complete his training in Italy. But Rembrandt must have been very well informed concerning the best of what was important in Italian painting; there was a very lively trade in prints between the different countries of Europe. Thus Rembrandt also knew the Italian predilection for portraits in profile, and perhaps he was even inspired by this when he painted this portrait in that fashion.

14. REMBRANDT VAN RIJN
Born 15th July 1606 at Leiden
Died 4th October 1669 at Amsterdam.

SASKIA VAN UYLENBURGH,
THE ARTIST'S WIFE
Wood, 99.5 cm. × 78.5 cm.
c. 1634.
Kassel, Staatliche Kunstsammlungen.

Samson, the strong man whom God had given to the Israelites to set them free from the Philistines, was betrayed by the Philistine woman Delilah. But Delilah was asked by the leaders of the Philistines to try to steal from Samson the secret of his strength. At first, Samson thought up many evasive answers, but finally he revealed the secret: if his hair were to be cut or shorn, then his strength would diminish. Delilah let Samson fall asleep with his head on her lap, and then shaved him bald. Then she called to the Philistines, who took Samson and put his eyes out. Now Samson had to turn a mill in prison.

This painting wholly follows the Italian tradition and that of the Dutch Caravaggists, painters who were really more Italian than the Italians themselves: dramatic in conception, contrasting light and shade, large in format.

Rembrandt gave this picture as a present to Constantijn Huygens in 1639. An unusual present indeed, a great, shocking scene like this; it is to be hoped, however, that Rembrandt had informed himself well concerning Huygens' taste. Rembrandt did not do such a thing without reason. He had, through Constantijn Huygens, acquired a commission from the Stadhouder Frederik Hendrik to supply five paintings of scenes from the Passion of Jesus (Alte Pinakothek, Munich). The delivery of these took place between 1636 and 1639. Rembrandt corresponded with Huygens about the delivery and payment. These seven letters are the only ones known by Rembrandt; they are not, alas, sources for learning to know Rembrandt the man; this correspondence is impersonal and strictly factual.

It was probably the accepted thing that a painter who obtained a large order like this should give the middle-man in the transaction a present. It could not have been Huygens' first present from a business transaction. What his reactions were on this gift, we do not, alas, know.

15. REMBRANDT VAN RIJN
Born 15th July 1606 at Leiden
Died 4th October 1669 at Amsterdam.

THE BLINDING OF SAMSON
"THE TRIUMPH OF DELILAH"
Canvas, 236 cm. × 302 cm.
signed and dated: 1636;
Frankfurt, Städelsches Kunstinstitut.

Danaë lay shut up in an underground room. Her father, Acrisius, king of Argos, had obtained the information from an oracle that the son of his daughter Danaë would kill him. To avoid that, he had shut up his daughter. But Zeus, the principal god of the Greeks, knew of a very good way round this: he visited Danaë disguised as golden rain, and so Perseus was born.

Even without travelling to Italy, Rembrandt was very well-informed of the predilection that his Italian colleagues had for the story of Danaë. Pictures of female nudes were, indeed, much more common in Italy: in the North, apart from Eve, only Susanna and Bathsheba, women of the Old Testament, had any attention bestowed on them. And the paintings were usually small in size. In his picture of Danaë, Rembrandt followed Italian taste completely: the painting is among the largest that Rembrandt ever executed. The bed, the old attendant, the cupid — these are absent from none of the Italian paintings. Rembrandt omitted only the golden rain which the Italians liked to include, generally shown in the form of golden coins. The little slippers by the bed are a typically Dutch attribute: in countless seventeenth-century paintings, they are an allusion to erotic happenings.

Rembrandt probably painted the Danaë in 1636 — the figure 3 in the date is rather indistinct. But X-ray photographs have revealed that Rembrandt, perhaps many years later, made a few alterations: Danaë's glance was directed more downwards, her ear-drops and the two ropes of pearls around her neck disappeared, the jewels on the little table by the bed were painted out, the old maidservant originally stood more to the left, with her face completely in profile. Perhaps all these alterations were made because Rembrandt had the painting in his house for a long time. For when an inventory of Rembrandt's possessions was drawn up in 1656, there was in the big studio on the first floor "a large likeness of Danaë". Was this a sculpture, another painting, or was it this Danaë? Who can tell?!

16. REMBRANDT VAN RIJN
Born 15th July 1606 at Leiden
Died 4th October 1669 at Amsterdam.

DANAË
Canvas, 185 cm. × 203 cm.
signed and dated: 16(3)6;
Leningrad, Hermitage.

Hercules Seghers was some sixteen years older than Rembrandt. He left Amsterdam as early as 1632, after he had had to sell his house there. In 1638, he died in The Hague, according to tradition, due to falling downstairs. So Rembrandt had only a small chance to really make contact with Seghers.

When, in connection with the declaration of Rembrandt's bankruptcy in 1656, the contents of his house, from top to bottom, were listed, there were various paintings — landscapes — by Hercules Seghers. That Rembrandt admired Seghers' work is clear; it is obvious too from the way in which he himself painted landscapes.

The appreciation of his work came too late for Seghers himself. When Samuel van Hoogstraten wrote about the art of his own time in 1678, he included Seghers' name in the chapter in which he discusses painters who were definitely not appreciated as was their due.

Only a few of Seghers' paintings are known. At present, these are all landscapes, although inventories record that he also painted very good still-lifes.

His landscapes are imaginary ones: he learnt from his master what the countryside outside Holland looked like, and this fascinated him. The Dutch countryside with its broad expanse of sky and flat land did not inspire him. Seghers is very closely related to the painters of the sixteenth century. They built up their landscapes rather like sets in the theatre: there was always a set-piece to the right and the left, to suggest depth. Towards the background, this kind of landscape became bluer and bluer, which always gave an appearance of depth.

But Seghers painted with much less precision than his predecessors: his rocks are suggestions of rocks, and a little village in the distance is only vaguely indicated.

17. HERCULES SEGHERS
Born 1589/1590 at Haarlem (?)
Died 1638 at The Hague.

A RIVER IN A VALLEY
Wood, 30 cm. × 53.5 cm.
signed;
Amsterdam, Rijksmuseum.

Rembrandt's landscapes were never pictures of scenes that really existed. Rembrandt was, witness his drawings and etchings, a keen walker in natural surroundings; his paintings might very well have been inspired by what he had seen. But at home in his studio, he wanted to make more of a painting than a memory of a certain spot.

Open nature was easily to be reached by the people of seventeenth-century Amsterdam. There was no talk of the layout of the great series of canals, the Herengracht, the Prinsengracht and the Keizersgracht, till the end of the seventeenth century; before that time, the Singel was the outermost boundary of the city. No one had to walk for any longer than ten minutes to reach one of the city-gates.

Rembrandt's great model in landscape-painting was Hercules Seghers. Like Seghers, Rembrandt himself was very free in his treatment of reality. But Seghers' landscapes were tranquil, static; Rembrandt's landscapes are dramatic, with strong variations of light and shade, as if a thunderstorm is near, with wild clouds and dense tree-shapes. Even though this landscape by Rembrandt is definitely a Dutch one, nothing in it makes us remember the grey, rustic landscapes of Rembrandt's contemporaries.

There are probably about ten people in this painting, busy with their daily occupations: on the way to the fields, waiting at an inn, walking and fishing, but they are unimportant in Rembrandt's nature.

18. REMBRANDT VAN RIJN
Born 15th July 1606 at Leiden
Died 4th October 1669 at Amsterdam.

THE STONE BRIDGE
Wood, 29.5 cm. × 42.5 cm.
c. 1638;
Amsterdam, Rijksmuseum.

The Trip family was a rich merchant family, of a class which could hardly really advance any further in Holland. They possessed iron-mines, arms factories and also had dealings in the money-trade. To have a commission from such a family was no small matter. Rembrandt himself had two commissions from the Amsterdam branch of the Trip family: one from Aletta Adriaensdochter, the widow of Elias Trip since 1631, and a second from Maria Trip, the daughter of Elias and Aletta. Rembrandt depicted her in all the glory of a rich merchant's daughter: she is wearing a very modern dress embellished with gold lace. The waist is high-set, and there is a flat collar and broad cuffs, both of which are similarly trimmed with lace; pearl ear-drops, pearl bracelets and a pearl necklace adorn the matt skin. Right in the background, which Rembrandt always kept as simple as possible, he placed an arch of rough stones. This gives the painting even more appeal. It is a fitting portrait of a girl who probably led the life of a princess in Amsterdam.

Moreover, she knew exactly how the portrait would turn out. Rembrandt had first made a drawing, and he must first have let his important employer see it.

Two years later, Maria Trip was married to the brother of her brother-in-law, Balthasar Coymans, a rich merchant; he was exactly thirty years older than she was. Her descendants still have her portrait in their possession, but in 1897 they sent it on loan to the Rijksmuseum.

19. REMBRANDT VAN RIJN
Born 15th July 1606 at Leiden
Died 4th October 1669 at Amsterdam.

MARIA TRIP (1619–1683)
Teak, 107 cm. × 82 cm.
signed and dated: 1639:
Amsterdam, Rijksmuseum,
on loan from the
Van Weede Foundation since 1897.

No-one really knows who painted this picture. At the moment, most people attribute it to Ferdinand Bol. Around 1900, no-one had any real doubt that it was a painting by Rembrandt.

The subject is Elisabeth Jacobsdochter Bas, the widow (since 1627) of lieutenant-admiral Jochem Swartenhont. Elisabeth Bas is wearing the dress of an important citizen's wife in the seventeenth century — the cutaway suit, a loose jacket which is open over an underdress of the same material; a jacket like that was often trimmed with fur. The stiff millstone collar was really a little out of fashion around 1640 and the winged cap too was worn only by older or more conservative women at the time. The handkerchief is represented in countless portraits, for the most part worn by older women.

All that we can make out about Elisabeth Bas from the painting is that she was then 70, or perhaps 75, so that her portrait is generally dated at around 1642, when she would have been some 71 years old. At that time, Ferdinand Bol did indeed paint portraits in a style which still very strongly resembled Rembrandt's manner of painting around 1635, when Ferdinand Bol was his pupil.

After 1640, Rembrandt was in the habit of painting more original, more unusual portraits; he moved further and further away from his style of painting at the time when Ferdinand Bol and Govert Flinck were his pupils. The pupils did the opposite: by continuing to embroider on what they learnt from Rembrandt, they became, in the course of time, more fashionable, more polished in that style. Around 1650, the difference between the portraits of the master and his pupils was so great that it could no longer be seen how there could ever have been a close connection between the two styles. Public taste ultimately opted for the work of Bol and his pupils; then Bol made a glittering career as a portrait-painter.

20. FERDINAND BOL
Baptised 24th June 1616 at Dordrecht
Buried 24th July 1680 at Amsterdam.

ELISABETH BAS (1571-1649)
Canvas, 118 cm. × 91.5 cm.
c. 1642;
Amsterdam, Rijksmuseum.

The rich Spanish merchant Alfonso Lopez was a fervent collector of Italian art. He lived in Amsterdam, where he was an agent of the French king and dealt in money and diamonds. He could certainly allow himself to spend a few on his collection. When, on the 9th April 1639, there took place the sale of the art-dealer Lucas van Uffelen's collection of Italian paintings, Lopez was there bidding for himself. What he acquired then was pretty good too: Raphael's portrait of Baldassare Castiglione (now in the Louvre, Paris). Rembrandt was also present at the sale: he made a sketch of the portrait and wrote beside it that the painting had become the property of Lopez for 3,500 florins.

Perhaps Rembrandt also visited Lopez at home, on the Singel, to see his collection, for another painting in the collection made a deep impression on Rembrandt: Titian's 'Portrait of Ludovico Ariosto' ('The Man in Blue', now in the National Gallery in London). Rembrandt then painted his own portrait as a sort of mixture of the two brilliant Italian portraits.

The light blue of the costume of Titian's 'Ariosto' was not Rembrandt's colour. But the pose suited him very well: the elbow resting on a stone ledge, the wide sleeve falling over it. Rembrandt chose to borrow the hat and the colours of the costume from the portrait of Castiglione by Raphael.

An impressive portrait of the 34-year-old painter. But then, Rembrandt was not just anyone in Amsterdam at that time: he had bought a large private house in 1639, was a popular master, a portrait-painter much in demand and the friend of all the high-ranking people in Amsterdam. The painter who had moved from Leiden to Amsterdam only nine years before had made a successful career!

21. REMBRANDT VAN RIJN
Born 15th July 1606 at Leiden
Died 4th October 1669 at Amsterdam.

SELF-PORTRAIT
AT THE AGE OF 34
Canvas, 102 cm. × 80 cm.
signed and dated: 1640;
London, National Gallery.

22. BARTHOLOMEUS VAN DER HELST
Born 1613 at Haarlem
Buried 16th December 1670
at Amsterdam.

THE ARCHERS' DINNER
AT THE PEACE OF MÜNSTER
Canvas, 232 cm. × 537 cm.
signed and dated: 1648;
Amsterdam, Rijksmuseum.

On the 18th June 1648, a great dinner was held in the quarters of the archers company at Sint Jorisdoelen, to celebrate the Peace of Münster. With the Peace — from the 16th May 1648 — the war between Spain and the Netherlands was finally, after 80 years, at an end. The painter Bartholomeus van der Helst was asked to immortalize this festivity. Van der Helst was a clever painter: with no apparent difficulty, he grouped people, combined colours, conscientiously detailed all the different faces. Certainly a painter who must greatly have pleased those who commissioned him: he forgot no little detail of their splendid festive dress.

Bartholomeus van der Helst was seven years younger than Rembrandt, but they were soon competing with each other. Anyone who wished to have his portrait painted in the '40s had to make the choice between the style of Rembrandt and that of Van der Helst. From Van der Helst, one always had a portrait that was extremely flattering and elegant; from Rembrandt, it would be a special portrait, whose like had not been painted before. For all that, many people seemed ultimately to prize elegance above originality.

Shortly after 1639, both Rembrandt and Van der Helst were asked to work on the embellishment of the banqueting hall of the 'Kloveniersdoelen' in Amsterdam. Rembrandt's former pupil Govert Flinck was also commissioned to work there. Thus the archers' hall was a sort of cross-section of what Amsterdam had to offer in the art of portrait-painting at the beginning of the 1640s.

The entry of the French queen-mother, Maria de' Medici into Amsterdam in 1638 was a great event for the companies of guards: they had ample opportunity to give 'acte-de-présence' at this time. Inspired by the pomp and the splendour, the archers of the 'Kloveniersdoelen' decided to embellish the banqueting-hall of their company with a series of paintings. Each company was to have a group-portrait painted; above the fireplace would be a group-portrait of the officers: the masters of the regiment.

Rembrandt's pupil Govert Flinck was given a commission, as was Bartholomeus van der Helst and also Rembrandt himself. The company under the command of Frans Banning Cocq went to Rembrandt to have their portrait painted: what they knew of his work corresponded apparently to their taste. Altogether, sixteen people paid for the painting, at the rate of 100 florins per head; as was the custom, some paid more, some less, depending on the position they would occupy in the painting.

In the family album of Frans Banning Cocq, there is a drawing of Rembrandt's group-portrait and beside it is written exactly what he wanted to put in the picture: "the young Junker Van Purmerlant, as the captain, is giving an order to his lieutenant, the Junker Van Vlaerdingen, to command the company of guards to march." Thus it was action that Rembrandt wanted; not a row of stiff, posing guards, as was often painted, but a group of men who are busy in action.

Rembrandt made his painting dark, for where there is darkness, light can be created: the girl with the hen in the middle, the golden yellow suit of Lieutenant Willem van Ruytenburch. But it was the very darkness that made people give the picture the name of "The Night Watch" in the eighteenth century, whereas Rembrandt really wanted to depict a group of guards who were setting out in daylight.

In 1715, archery was given up in Amsterdam, and the company quarters, with their contents, became the property of the municipality of Amsterdam. Shortly after that, the guards' effects were brought across to the Town Hall in the Dam. There was a place reserved for "The Night Watch" between two doors, but it was rather too small for the painting. The city restorer had, much to his regret, to make the painting smaller on all four sides.

23. REMBRANDT VAN RIJN
Born 15th July 1606 at Leiden
Died 4th October 1669 at Amsterdam.

"THE NIGHT WATCH"
THE MILITIA COMPANY
OF CAPTAIN FRANS BANNING
COCQ AND LIEUTENANT
WILLEM VAN RUYTENBURCH
Canvas, 359 cm. × 438 cm.
signed and dated: 1642;
Amsterdam, Rijksmuseum.

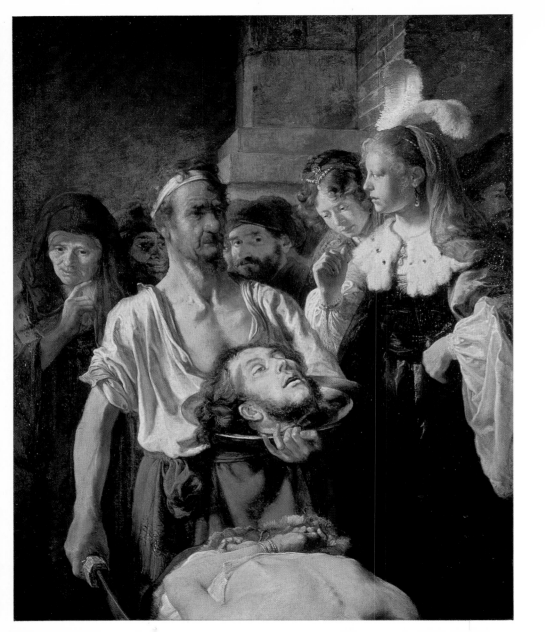

The father of Carel Fabritius was a schoolteacher in Midden Beemster, a little village in the neighbourhood of Amsterdam. In his free time, he painted quite a lot. His son Carel became a carpenter, and because of this, he later called himself Fabritius in Amsterdam (faber = carpenter). For all that, Carel finally opted for the profession of painter: in 1641, he became a pupil of Rembrandt's in Amsterdam, for the length of about a year. In 1650, he moved to Delft with his wife. He perished there on the explosion of the ammunition depot on the 12th October 1654.

When the Rijksmuseum bought this painting in 1801, it was thought to be a Rembrandt, the first Rembrandt in the museum. However, towards the middle of the 19th century, the name Rembrandt was taken off, and it was ascribed to two of Rembrandt's pupils: Carel Fabritius and Govert Flinck. It is obvious that Rembrandt must have had something to do with the painting: the colours, the play of light, the expressions on the faces remind one strongly of Rembrandt's work. It was, furthermore, probably painted at the time when Rembrandt was at work on 'The Night Watch': this painting and 'The Night Watch' have in common a way of placing all the people one behind another.

All of Rembrandt's pupils were still painting very much in the style of their master shortly after the termination of their training. No work done by Fabritius shortly after 1642 is really known, unless we assume that in the "Beheading of John the Baptist" we do indeed have an example of the manner in which Rembrandt's pupil Fabritius, who had just finished his training, was putting into practice the lessons of his master.

It is clear from Fabritius' later work that he was really the only pupil of Rembrandt's who could attain to the same standard as his master. His early death robbed him of the chance to really prove that.

The story of this picture is that of Salome. Salome, the daughter of King Herod, had danced so beautifully before her father and his guests that she was granted a wish. Influenced by her mother, she asked for, and obtained, the head of her father's prisoner, John the Baptist, and she had it presented to her on a silver plate.

24. CAREL FABRITIUS (?)
*Baptised 27th February 1622
at Midden-Beemster
Died 12th October 1654 at Delft.*

THE BEHEADING OF
JOHN THE BAPTIST
*Canvas, 149 cm. × 121 cm.
c. 1642;
Amsterdam. Rijksmuseum.*

The "all is vanity" with which the Preacher in the Old Testament begins his account, was an oft-quoted piece of wisdom in university circles in Leiden. The transitoriness of life — and also of knowledge — was an awareness that did not, it is true, make men too sad, but it formed an essential part of any thinking which was concerned with the actions of men. In that milieu in Leiden, there appeared, around 1625, the vanitas (= vanity) still-lifes. All things concerned with the temporary nature of man, his thoughts and acts were assembled in these: old books, musical instruments, flowers which were withering, fruit going rotten, clocks ticking away the time, skulls, a burning — or even blown-out — candle.

Vanitas still-lifes quickly became a reliable genre for painters. When Rembrandt's inventory was drawn up in 1656, it mentioned as many as three vanitas still-lifes by Rembrandt himself.

In this painting, the vanitas still-life is combined with another essentially Dutch kind of still-life, the "breakfast", composed of what was required for a simple meal.

X-ray photographs have shown that there have been three painters at work on this panel, one after another. The panel came first into the hands of a portrait-painter, who painted on it a portrait of a woman in a simple dark-coloured dress with a white collar, probably shortly after 1625. Then came the still-life painter, who turned the panel on its side and painted over the portrait of the woman a vanitas still-life with old books, a globe, a palette and brushes: so transitory is all art and science. That still-life is so like the work of Rembrandt shortly before his journey from Leiden to Amsterdam, that this painter has been called — albeit somewhat hesitantly — Rembrandt. Then came the third painter and he skilfully painted, over the corner of the stone table-top, a 'breakfast', a pewter jug, a glass, a pewter plate and a roll. It is not at present known who did this.

25. REMBRANDT VAN RIJN (?)
Born 15th July 1606 at Leiden
Died 4th October 1669 at Amsterdam.

STILL-LIFE WITH VANITAS-SYMBOLS
Wood, 91 cm. × 120 cm.
c. 1630;
Amsterdam, Rijksmuseum.

Dordrecht was an important trading-centre in the seventeenth century: it was the stores market for everything that was transported further by river. There were also numerous contacts between Dordrecht and Amsterdam, the largest port in Holland. In 1641, Samuel van Hoogstraten came from Dordrecht to be a pupil of Rembrandt's. At the time, Van Hoogstraten knew everything about the work of painters: from his seventh year, he had learnt how to paint from his father, who was also a painter. When the latter died in 1641, Samuel made the great step to Amsterdam. Van Hoogstraten stayed with Rembrandt for three years. Only in 1644 could he sign his own work, as during his training a pupil's work was the property of his master. The work of Rembrandt made a great impression on Van Hoogstraten. He was only 15 or 16 then. Later, he went on his travels, to Vienna, to Rome, to London. Then Rembrandt's lessons seemed to be forgotten.

This painting is one of the first that Van Hoogstraten made as an independent painter. Rembrandt must have told him about the vanitas still-lifes in Leiden. In any case, Van Hoogstraten also assembled all the recognized symbols for his painting: books, an hour-glass, a skull, a burnt-out candle. Even the young man seems to be all too imbued with the 'vanity' of the title. Rembrandt and his pupils were not very interested in mere still-lifes; man was what they were concerned with. This painting has, indeed, been called a self-portrait. But so long as it remains unknown what the young Samuel van Hoogstraten looked like, it is not possible to affirm that this really is a self-portrait.

Much more important than Van Hoogstraten's artistic offerings is the book he had published in 1678: "Introduction to the High Art of Painting". In it, all kinds of questions concerning the art of his time come up for discussion. What he writes about Rembrandt, for example, he based on his own observations.

26. SAMUEL VAN HOOGSTRATEN
Born 2nd August 1627 at Dordrecht
Died 19th October 1678 at Dordrecht.

A YOUNG MAN AT A TABLE
WITH VANITAS-SYMBOLS
"SELF-PORTRAIT WITH
VANITAS STILL-LIFE"
Wood, 58 cm. × 74 cm.
signed and dated: 1644;
Rotterdam,
Boymans-Van Beuningen Museum.

In the Republic of the United Netherlands, religious pictures were not normally painted for the — Protestant — Church, but just for private individuals. In Holland, therefore, such pictures are often homely, intimate and cosy. Indeed, they never had the drama of the pictures painted by Italian religious artists, for example.

In this painting, Rembrandt uses a very old Christian theme: the trinity of St. Anne. Anne, the mother of Mary, Mary herself, and the child Jesus close to them. In old Italian paintings, Mary and the child Jesus are often sitting right on St. Anne's lap. Rembrandt uses this theme rather without the deep symbolism which is essentially part of it. He makes of it a homely scene, which is situated in an ordinary Dutch interior. Even Joseph may be present, though in the darkness, half hidden under the staircase. This time, Rembrandt has included the source of light in his picture, but in such a way that only the effects of the light are visible: particularly the great protective shadow of St. Anne.

A contractor would be not a little astonished if he were to be given a commission to construct one of Rembrandt's interiors. What looks like a rather strange but very realistic room is in fact not very substantial. Rembrandt was never interested in really authentic-looking architecture. And this was at a time when many of his contemporaries — Pieter Saenredam, Gerrit Berckheyde, Emanuel de Witte — painted pictures with interiors and exteriors so realistically that these could be of help in present-day restoration projects. Rembrandt depicted children as no other painter has done. And this was in the seventeenth century, when the notion of a child as a very special kind of being scarcely existed.

Three of the children of Rembrandt and Saskia died shortly after birth. Only Titus, who was born in 1641, survived to adulthood. Rembrandt could make as many drawings and studies of his only child as he wanted to.

27. REMBRANDT VAN RIJN
Born 15th July 1606 at Leiden
Died 4th October 1669 at Amsterdam.

THE HOLY FAMILY
Wood, 66.3 cm. × 78 cm.
c. 1644;
Amsterdam, Rijksmuseum.

Three days had passed since Jesus' crucifixion. On the first morning after the Sabbath, a few women went to watch by his grave, but it was empty. They saw only two angels and these said that Jesus was no longer dead, but had risen. The women quickly told the great news to the diciples, but they thought it an improbable story.

Since the events of these days, two followers of Jesus who were on the way from Jerusalem to the little village of Emmaus had been travelling for two hours. On the way, they were joined by a stranger. Naturally they told him everything that had happened in Jerusalem during the last few days. Then the stranger told them that it had all been written by Moses and the prophets that the Messiah must first suffer before he could attain to a state of blessedness.

When they arrived at Emmaus, the two men asked the stranger to stay with them and eat with them. And then, as he broke the bread and spoke the blessing, the men saw clearly that the stranger was Jesus himself. And, with that, he disappeared. Rembrandt chose for his painting that moment in which the two men suddenly recognize Jesus. The men sit rigid: they cannot believe their own eyes. Only the servant notices nothing, but then he has no knowledge of what has happened in Jerusalem.

Rembrandt put his Christ in front of a sort of niche in a simple romanesque church. A bare, unadorned church, moreover, for this was the kind of church Rembrandt knew. Since Protestantism had become the official religion in the Republic, decoration of the churches was taboo. Rembrandt painted many studies of the head of Christ: in his inventory of 1656, there is even mention of a 'Head of Christ after the life'. Obviously Rembrandt just used one of the many Jewish people who lived near him as a model.

28. REMBRANDT VAN RIJN
Born 15th July 1606 at Leiden
Died 4th October 1669 at Amsterdam.

CHRIST AT EMMAUS
Wood. 68 cm. × 85 cm.
signed and dated: 1648;
Paris, Louvre.

On the long list of Rembrandt's possessions, drawn up on the 25th and 26th July 1656, there is mentioned among other things, a "carbaedse helmet". What this word "carbaedse" means exactly, no one knows. It was thought to be "Carpathian", though no one knew exactly what such a helmet should look like. It has also been read as "carbaedse", which would then mean Caribbean. We now know that the Spaniards were particularly fond of the work of the goldsmiths of the Caribbean region, particularly those of Mexico. They brought it in large quantities to Europe and even copied it themselves.

But Rembrandt never had the intention of making his paintings 'material for archaeologists'. It can never be proved for sure what kind of helmet the man in the painting has on, or whether the painting is identical with the "carbaedse helmet" of Rembrandt's inventory. That the helmet was painted from the life seems certain, as the reflections of light are so realistically rendered. It was, moreover, a fine object for someone like Rembrandt, who was keen on effects of light and shade and shades of gold.

The head of the man is really more interesting than the helmet, with the deep lines in his face and his hard mouth; he is deeply sunk in himself eternally.

Rembrandt is, indeed, the only seventeenth-century artist who painted a large number of pictures which apparently have no meaning: they are not portraits, not portrayals of an important biblical or historical character. It seems that they were painted just because the master was fascinated by a certain face, by a certain object, by the interplay between them.

It might well be even that Rembrandt, apart from the paintings that were commissioned, dealt in his own and other artists' paintings. That conclusion could be drawn from the fact that in 1656 the painter had a lot more pictures by other masters in his possession, and also from the fact that after his bankruptcy in 1656, Titus and Hendrickje set up an art-dealer's business together, and therefore Rembrandt had to work for board and lodging.

A picture like this one could have been painted for the business, for people who did not buy a painting for its content, but because they were unexpectedly struck by a man in a golden helmet.

29. REMBRANDT VAN RIJN
Born 15th July 1606 at Leiden
Died 4th October 1669 at Amsterdam.

"THE MAN WITH THE
GOLDEN HELMET"
Canvas, 67 cm. × 50 cm.
c. 1648;
Berlin-Dahlem, Gemäldegalerie.

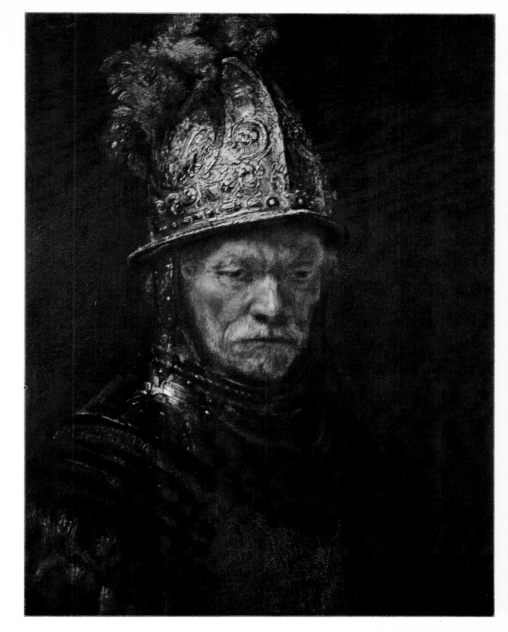

It can be seen from this painting how difficult it is to find out the ups and downs in an artist's life regarding his work.

Up to 1928, it was thought that this self-portrait was dated 1656. And it was thought that the man there looked depressed. The painting was a symbol of the great drama in Rembrandt's life that culminated in 1656: the declaration of his insolvency, the sale of all his possessions, his house, his paintings, drawings and etchings, his removal to a small, simple house on the Rozengracht.

But on the restoration of the painting in 1928, it appeared that the portrait was not dated 1656, but 1652. Then — in 1652 — there was as yet no talk of bankruptcy: Rembrandt still had plenty of important commissions. And so the portrait of a depressed artist became one of a proud and successful painter, who "whenever he was working, would not have received a king".

Exactly as the romanticised biographies tell us, Rembrandt was unwilling to go to receive visitors: creditors, people bringing commissions, with their too-complicated wishes, people in high positions, for whom he had no time.

This self-portrait is very unusual, as a self-portrait by Rembrandt, but also in general, as that of a seventeenth-century painter. The work seems to retreat before us, without finery, without a pose.

Originally, when it was a little broader, this painting must have been even more impressive than it is now: both of Rembrandt's elbows were included. The painting was later shortened on the sides.

30. REMBRANDT VAN RIJN
Born 15th July 1606 at Leiden
Died 4th October 1669 at Amsterdam.

SELF-PORTRAIT
Canvas. 112 cm. × 81.5 cm.
signed and dated: 1652;
Vienna, Kunsthistorisches Museum.

When, in 1631, Rembrandt moved to Amsterdam from Leiden for good, his pupil Gerard Dou stayed behind there. Dou quickly became the leading painter in Leiden, a position which Rembrandt otherwise would have probably occupied.

Leiden was, after Amsterdam, the most important city in Holland; the Leiden cloth-industry continued to become more important and brought a lot of money in its wake. And where there is money, there is also a wide market for paintings. The work of Dou was much to the taste of the people of Leiden, for his paintings were very finely executed, small in format and fitted so well into small, well cared-for houses in Leiden.

Perhaps Dou did sometimes hear about the successes that his former master had in Amsterdam. But similar as their work had been when they were both working together in the same studio, it was as different again some ten years afterwards. Dou's most popular and most salable compositions were those which depicted one or more figures posed in a stone window-frame. And the alcove was always embellished differently, with a curtain, a carpet, bunches of grapes. No wonder then that Dou also posed for his self-portrait in such a stone recess, really rather as though he were just looking out at the viewers through a frame. The Leiden painters were very keen on 'trompe l'œil' and even thought it very amusing. Hence the dog-eared little piece of paper with Dou's name on it, and also his name carved on the window-sill. That is also why he hangs a little green curtain half-drawn across the window. That was often done in the seventeenth century: paintings were protected from the effect of the light by a green curtain. And painters such as Dou and his pupils, who wanted to paint "with nice precision", were sure always to hang a little curtain like this one in front of their paintings.

31. GERARD DOU
Born 7th April 1613 at Leiden
Buried 9th February 1675 at Leiden.

SELF-PORTRAIT
Wood, 48 cm. × 37 cm.
signed. c. 1645;
Amsterdam, Rijksmuseum.

Dordrecht was the birthplace of many important painters in the seventeenth century. Albert Cuyp was born there, Samuel van Hoogstraten, and, in 1634, Nicolaes Maes. Yet, for the people of Dordrecht, Amsterdam remained the Mecca for the training of painters. So Nicolaes Maes also went to Amsterdam, and in about 1648, he became Rembrandt's pupil. That meant that he made payments of some 100 florins per year, and had in return board and lodging, in addition to his training as a painter of course. In addition to this, Maes would be more or less obliged to spend a period of three years as Rembrandt's pupil. But what his style of painting was like when Rembrandt passed him as a master-painter is not known. We know only work of his dating from 1653, the year in which Maes returned to Dordrecht to live. He hardly ever dated his paintings and that makes it almost impossible to have a clear picture of the development of his work.

Back in Dordrecht, Maes painted genre-pictures exclusively, with women doing their work, busy spinning or watching by a cradle, or plucking a chicken. These paintings hardly recall the work of the master Rembrandt.

Maes' "Old woman praying" is a very distinctive painting. He has depicted the objects with a very observant clarity — the pottery, the loaves of bread, the knife, the keys, the funnel, the hour-glass — with much consideration for the appearance of every object. The old woman is also depicted as being so still, that this painting could almost be called a still-life, were it not for the cat, made greedy by the smell of fish and suddenly showing signs of life. The effect of light and shade is, perhaps, what Maes had learnt from Rembrandt.

32. NICOLAES MAES
Born January 1634 at Dordrecht
Buried 24th December 1693
at Amsterdam.

AN OLD WOMAN PRAYING
"THE ENDLESS PRAYER"
Canvas. 134 cm. × 113 cm.
signed, c. 1655;
Amsterdam, Rijksmuseum.

The reputation of Rembrandt spread far across frontiers. The rich Sicilian art-collector, Don Antonio Ruffo, conceived the idea of hanging a series of portraits of famous men in his library. He sent a request to the Dutch painter Rembrandt van Rijn to paint the portrait of a philosopher for the series. It is not known whether Ruffo himself stipulated that the philosopher had to be Aristotle. For a Dutchman, the choice would be a very easy one. Aristotle was *the* classical philosopher in Holland, education in the philosophy of Aristotle being a compulsory subject in Dutch universities. In 1654, Rembrandt's painting was finished and shipped off to Messina. A year earlier, Rembrandt had received his honorarium of 500 florins from Ruffo. A large amount, in the opinion of the latter: an Italian painter would never ask so much.

Rembrandt portrayed Aristotle in a particular function: as the tutor of Alexander the Great, to whom he had taught the art of war by using quotations from Homer. That is why Aristotle's hand is resting on a bust of Homer, and that is also why he is wearing on his breast a medal with the image of Alexander, on a golden chain.

For the bust of Homer, Rembrandt probably painted the plaster cast that he had — as the inventory of 1656 again shows — in his studio. Rembrandt also had a bust of Aristotle, but what it looked like and whether the artist used it for his painting is not known. In any case, Aristotle's costume is not classical. It is the costume in which scholars were depicted, even in the sixteenth century: a wide, light-coloured gown, a dark garment worn over it, a large hat.

Ruffo gave other commissions for his gallery of famous men: to the Italian painters Guercino and Mattia Preti, and later, again to Rembrandt: for portraits of Alexander and Homer. Only the latter painting has been preserved — though damaged by fire — in the Mauritshuis at The Hague. The later contact between Rembrandt and Ruffo was somewhat less amicable than before: Ruffo found great fault with what the painter sent him from Holland. The business was never settled to the satisfaction of both.

33. REMBRANDT VAN RIJN
Born 15th July 1606 at Leiden
Died 4th October 1669 at Amsterdam.

ARISTOTLE CONTEMPLATING
A BUST OF HOMER
Canvas, 139 cm. × 133 cm.
signed and dated: 1653;
New York, Metropolitan Museum.

The grandfather of Jan Six had founded a large cloth- and silk-weaving business in Amsterdam. And even his grandson was thereby ensured a livelihood with few financial problems.

In 1652, Jan Six decided to withdraw from the weaving business as a partner, intending to devote himself only to the administrative duties to be done from then on. And to his hobbies: collecting art and writing poetry. In 1691, Six was Mayor of Amsterdam for a year; he was then just 73 years old.

Rembrandt delivered work to Six on several different occasions: in 1647, he made an etching of the young Jan Six, standing by a window with a book in his hand. In 1648, Rembrandt made an etching which was to be used as the title-page for Jan Six's play "Medea". The etching represents the marriage of Jason and Creusa.

In 1654, Rembrandt painted this portrait of Jan Six. A year earlier, the master had borrowed money from Six, in order to be able to pay the previous owner of his house in Breestraat the last instalment of the sale price. Six's portrait was therefore probably also a paying off of the debt in kind. Rembrandt very often did that: he paid people with etchings or paintings.

Buth nothing of the debtor-creditor relationship is apparent in the portrait. This is Rembrandt at his best: a fascinating delineation of the face, an attractive attitude.

It is known from a poem by Six that the picture was painted in 1654: in a short Latin text, Six worked in Roman numerals that together form the date 1654.

Tradition has it that there existed a close friendship between Jan Six and Rembrandt, that their contact with each other was more than was usual in business relationships between an art-collector and an artist. There is no reliable proof at all for this assumption.

34. REMBRANDT VAN RIJN
Born 15th July 1606 at Leiden
Died 4th October 1669 at Amsterdam.

JAN SIX (1618-1700)
Canvas, 112 cm. × 102 cm.
Painted in 1654;
Amsterdam. Six Collection.

The only real travelling that Rembrandt ever did was to make a trip to Gelderland: he made some drawings there. He had never really seen the non-Dutch kind of landscapes that he often depicted in his paintings. He could picture to himself what mountainous scenery looked like, because he knew the work of colleagues who really had been abroad, to Italy. With what he learnt from his own observations, and what he had seen in others' work, and with buildings borrowed from prints, Rembrandt made his own imaginary landscapes.

He never chose a bright, sunny day, nor the normal hazy, grey Dutch atmosphere; he always chose the half-light of a sunrise, a sunset, a storm or approaching bad weather. That gave him the opportunity to make his landscapes dramatic, to play with the lighting effect.

Rembrandt certainly saw the boat in the background with the red, white and blue flag at home in Amsterdam, and also the bridge; that is the sort of bridge of which many were built in seventeenth-century Holland. But he probably borrowed the structure half-way up the hill (it is rather like a somewhat ruined amphitheatre) from pictures with ancient ruins.

How and what pupils painted during the time they were pupils is only seldom known, because they could not sign their works at this time. It must, after all, be definitely acknowledged that master and pupil often worked together on one painting. According to the seventeenth-century conception of the workshop, there was no objection to this at all. It could very well be, for example, that the horseman and the fisherman by the water's edge, who both appear rather crudely executed, were not painted by Rembrandt, but by a pupil.

35. REMBRANDT VAN RIJN
Born 15th July 1606 at Leiden
Died 4th October 1669 at Amsterdam.

LANDSCAPE WITH RUINS
Wood, 67 cm. × 87.5 cm.
signed, c. 1654;
Kassel, Staatliche Kunstsammlungen.

Philips Koninck was born in Amsterdam, but his father, a rich goldsmith, had him taught how to paint in Rotterdam. When Philips came back to Amsterdam in 1641, he was a fully-trained painter. It seems therefore highly improbable that he became a pupil of Rembrandt's. Yet Philips Koninck's own work shows so much influence of landscape-paintings by Hercules Seghers and Rembrandt, that he must at least have known their work well. But, unlike Rembrandt, with his imaginary landscapes, and Seghers, with his quite un-Dutch landscapes, Koninck preferred the flat Dutch countryside, the country in the south of Holland, usually with big rivers. Apart from being a painter, Koninck was also the owner of a business that ferried goods by ship from Amsterdam to Rotterdam and vice versa. He must therefore often have had work to do near the great rivers.

Although Philips Koninck's landscapes really do seem to be 'painted from life', a seventeenth-century artist never painted directly from nature. He went out with his sketchbook and drew in it exactly what he saw. But at home — in the studio — he combined the drawings into a painting as ideal and complete as he wished.

Koninck was not at all concerned with colour. He 'worked' with his paint: thick layers of paint gave form to the houses and trees in the landscape, but very thin, transparent little strokes gave the sky that very rarefied effect that all the grey and white clouds really did have.

Roelant Roghman earned his living as a drawer of castles and country-houses. He made regular journeys into the provinces and came back with piles of drawings destined for publishers of topographical works. But Roghman also painted. It is not known where he learnt to paint; of the whole span of his life, we have found no more information than he was probably born in Amsterdam in 1597 and certainly died there in 1686, in a poor-house. And we know that, together with Gerbrand van den Eeckhout, he was one of Rembrandt's best friends.

Roghman painted landscapes which rather recall Hercules Seghers: the same mountains and rock-formations, the same ravines. But whether Seghers and Roghman knew each other or not is an open question. That Roghman later came into contact with Rembrandt and Philips Koninck seems — from the evidence of his paintings — probable. Perhaps the slightly older Roghman was the very person who inspired the two others. Alas, Roghman never dated his paintings at all. No one has yet been successful enough to determine even approximately when the rocky landscapes were painted. That makes the answer to the question of who influenced whom even more uncertain.

Amazingly enough, not a single painting by Roelant Roghman is mentioned in Rembrandt's inventory of 1656.

37. ROELANT ROGHMAN
Born 1597 in Amsterdam
Died 1686 in Amsterdam.

LANDSCAPE WITH A FISHERMAN
Canvas, 80.5 cm. × 100 cm.
signed;
Amsterdam, Rijksmuseum.

One day, King David saw from the roof of his palace a very beautiful woman bathing. He enquired what the name of the woman was, and was told: that is Bathsheba, the wife of Uriah. David sent for her to come to him, and had intercourse with her. Later, he was to send her husband into the heat of battle, where he perished.

Practically every painter who ever depicts the story of Bathsheba chooses the moment when David espied her bathing. But not Rembrandt. His choice fell on the moment of Bathsheba's inner conflict: should she obey the command of the king — which carried great weight in those times — or should she remain faithful to her husband?

X-ray photographs revealed a short time ago that Bathsheba originally held her head high with self-assurance. After that, Rembrandt opted for the bowing of her head in pensive melancholy, as she gazes at the pedicurist at work.

There are quite a lof of drawings which tell us of the naked women who obviously used to pose as models for Rembrandt and his pupils. They are not ethereally beautiful women, but very ordinary Dutch women, who could put to good use the money earned by posing as a model. But Rembrandt also had prints in his collection taken from paintings of his Italian counterparts, who depicted extremely beautiful women on their canvases. Rembrandt made his Bathsheba somewhere between the two sorts of woman, ordinary and yet extraordinary. A large female nude like this was, moreover, an extremely unusual subject in Dutch painting.

38. REMBRANDT VAN RIJN
Born 15th July 1606 at Leiden
Died 4th October 1669 at Amsterdam.

BATHSHEBA
WITH DAVID'S LETTER
Canvas, 142 cm. × 142 cm.
signed and dated: 1654;
Paris, Louvre.

A few pictures is practically all the knowledge we have of Willem Drost: one painting bears the date 1653, two have the date 1654, and one is perhaps dated 1663. And there is a painting on which is written part of his Christian name: Wilhelm (a shortened form of Wilhelmus, the Latin form of Willem). But the most important information still comes from Arnold Houbraken's "Great Survey of Dutch Art...", in which it is stated that there was a painter called Drost who was a pupil of Rembrandt's. One assumes that must have been around 1650.

Just as Rembrandt did, Drost chose the character of Bathsheba as the subject for a painting in 1654. And he also took from the story the moment when Bathsheba has read the letter in which David asks her to come to him. But what a difference in treatment!

Looking at Rembrandt's Bathsheba, one is inclined to forgive the woman in anticipation for the decision she is going to make, because there is so much inner struggle in making the decision. Drost's Bathsheba is absolutely the charming little person who has attracted David: no inner conflict here, but something of a slight triumph that the king has chosen her.

Yet it seems probable that the two artists saw each other's work: the two paintings are so similar in composition, in the juxtaposition of colours, in costumes. The master-pupil relationship must then have been at an end, for Drost could sign his own work and was recognized as a fully-trained painter.

39. WILLEM DROST
Active from c. 1650 to c. 1665,
Born c. 1630,
Died c. 1687.

BATHSHEBA
WITH DAVID'S LETTER
Canvas, 101 cm. × 86 cm.
signed and dated: 1654;
Paris, Louvre.

From 1793 till 1910, this painting was in a collection in Poland, and since then it has been called "The Polish Rider". But between the year of the painting of the picture, about 1655, and its being bought out of Holland in 1793, there are almost 150 years: too much to say that this painting does really represent a Polish rider.

Although a contemporary of Rembrandt's praised him for the historical exactness in the costumes in his pictures, more recent examinations have shown very clearly that Rembrandt was not so faithful to the truth as his contemporary thought. It is even questionable whether historical knowledge in Rembrandt's time had advanced far enough for Rembrandt to dress his characters authentically — had he wanted to. But Rembrandt did not intend to do that at all. He was content to give an impression of an oriental or historical costume.

That makes it highly improbable that anyone will ever succeed completely in ascribing the costume of "The Polish Rider" to a certain district, a certain period, or even to a certain person.

Rembrandt obviously wanted to depict one or another of the oriental heroes. In the landscape in the background he put the sort of buildings that he also showed in Jerusalem. He dressed the man in a coat, a 'jupon', which had been used in representational art for the costume of oriental characters since the fifteenth century; a tight coat fastened to the waist with a lot of buttons, then falling open in tails. Perhaps the arms were copied from some in the collection shown in his studio inventory. The headgear is more like Rembrandt's favourite, the turban, than the fur cap which a "Polish Rider" should really have worn.

Whoever this young horseman really is, Rembrandt made a brilliant painting of him. The brown hills and little buildings in the background frame the colourfully-dressed figure excellently; a shaft of light falls on his back and lights up his coloured saddle-cloth and his jacket more fully. The horse is not standing still, but depicted in movement, as though the horseman is about to disappear from the picture.

40. REMBRANDT VAN RIJN
Born 15th July 1606 at Leiden
Died 4th October 1669 at Amsterdam.

THE POLISH RIDER
Canvas, 117 cm. × 135 cm.
Remains of a signature, c. 1655;
New York, The Frick Collection.

Titus van Rijn was born in 1641. He was the only one of the children of Saskia and Rembrandt who did not die shortly after birth. But a year after his birth, his mother Saskia did die. Nannies were then brought into the house for Titus: first Geertje Dirckx, with whom Rembrandt quarrelled and came to blows after a time, and, about 1649, Hendrickje Stoffels. She stayed with Titus and his father till her death in 1662.

It is not officially known what Titus looked like; no drawing or painting has the annotation: this is Titus. But it is very probable that the boy, and later the young man, with the thin white face and curly brown hair is Titus: he is represented again and again in paintings, always at an age which corresponds to Titus' age. For a long time, the paintings were not always real portraits: Titus sat as a model for the depiction of a certain subject, sometimes Rembrandt was pleasantly struck by a certain attitude. The last of these is the present one. Titus also wanted to be a painter. He must often have sat like this by his father in the studio: pen in hand, pen-case dangling beside the desk, gazing pensively before him over the drawing-board. No work by Titus van Rijn is known now; there were some in Rembrandt's inventory of 1656, and also in other archives, but what the standard of these was is not known.

Titus would be fourteen years old here. In that age, boys who had decided to be painters most often went as pupil to a master. But it was not to be a carefree training for Titus. The year after this, all his father's possessions had to be sold, even the work that Titus had done. And a few years later still, he had to apply for a declaration of majority, in order to set up an art-dealer's business with Hendrickje: because of guild regulations, Rembrandt himself was no longer able to sell his own works, as this was not allowed to artists who had been declared to be insolvent.

41. REMBRANDT VAN RIJN
Born 15th July 1606 at Leiden
Died 4th October 1669 at Amsterdam.

TITUS VAN RIJN (1641 - 1668),
SON OF THE PAINTER
"TITUS AT THE READING DESK"
Canvas, 77 cm. × 63 cm.
signed and dated: 1655;
Rotterdam,
Boymans-Van Beuningen Museum.

42. NICOLAES MAES
Born January 1634 at Dordrecht
Buried 24th December 1693
at Amsterdam.

THE PENSIVE GIRL
Canvas, 123 cm. × 96 cm.
signed, c. 1655;
Amsterdam, Rijksmuseum.

On the return journey to his birthplace Dordrecht after the termination of his training with Rembrandt, Maes may perhaps have visited certain other centres for artists: Leiden, where Gerard Dou was the great painter and Delft, where Carel Fabritius, a pupil of Rembrandt's, worked and where the star of Johannes Vermeer was just beginning to rise. Perhaps the impressions he received there made him forget a little what he had learnt from Rembrandt. In any case, the subjects that he usually painted, back in Dordrecht, seem to be clearly influenced by the work of the masters in Leiden and Delft: women indoors about their daily tasks.

Yet this painting still has some kinship with pictures which Rembrandt was painting around 1650: girls leaning on a window-sill.

But the similarity stops there: Maes painted smoothly and without emotion. The colours are attractive: a brilliant combination of orange, green and brown. The attitude of the girl is carefully thought out. Despite Maes' care, it is not really a living painting.

Peaches and apricots did in fact grow in Holland in the seventeenth century. Not in the same abundance as in a sub-tropical climate, but what Maes depicted here is not really so unusual as it seems now.

Just as Dr. Tulp had his public anatomy lesson painted by Rembrandt in 1632 (plate 12), so his successor, Dr. Joan Deyman also wanted to have that done. On the 29th January 1656, Dr. Deyman demonstrated an — unknown — aspect of the structure of the brain, using the corpse of a felon who had been hanged.

Dr. Deyman's picture was to be much larger than that of Dr. Tulp. Rembrandt later recorded in a little sketch what the picture looked like: how the figures were arranged and what sort of framework there was to the whole composition. The little drawing is now, alas, the only means of obtaining an impression of Rembrandt's 'Anatomy Lesson of Dr. Deyman'. For in 1723, fire ravaged the Theatrum Anatomicum in the Weighing House. Only about a quarter of Deyman's anatomical lesson was spared: the part with the corpse and the assistant Gijsbert Calcoen, who is holding the top of the skull in his hand. The figure of Dr. Deyman and those of the listeners were lost.

Rembrandt's second anatomical lesson is much more daring than the first: it was also 25 years later in date. He painted the corpse as seen from the front of it, foreshortened — by no means an easy task! He placed Dr. Deyman directly behind it, with the group of spectators symmetrically around it. It was, in essence, a composition which could appear rather stiff, but Rembrandt certainly knew how to make a lively whole out of it.

Though 1656 was the year of Rembrandt's bankruptcy, it was also the year in which he was given this commission by the Surgeons' Guild; truly an official confirmation of the enduring importance of Rembrandt as an artist.

43. REMBRANDT VAN RIJN
Born 15th July 1606 at Leiden
Died 4th October 1669 at Amsterdam.

THE ANATOMY LESSON
OF DR. JOAN DEYMAN
Canvas, 100 cm. × 134 cm.
signed and dated: 1656;
Amsterdam, Rijksmuseum.

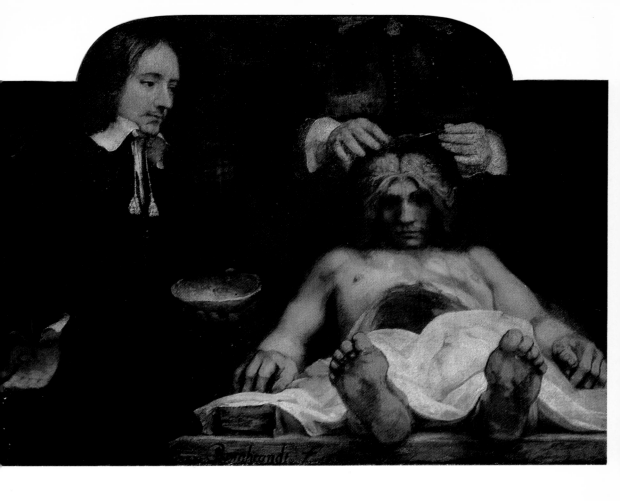

Many years before Rembrandt depicted the story of the blessing of the sons of Joseph by Jacob, his pupil Govert Flinck painted the blessing of Jacob by Isaac.

Isaac had two sons, twins: Esau and Jacob. Jacob grew up to be a home-loving man and Esau became a hunter of game. Father Isaac found this very pleasant, since he was very fond indeed of roast game. But Mother Rebecca was more fond of Jacob, the gentler son. Isaac became old and blind, and felt his end approaching. Then he called to Esau and asked him to go and shoot down some tasty game for him once again. Afterwards he would give Esau his blessing. Rebecca heard the conversation between father and son. She quickly prepared an appetising meal with a billy-goat from the herd, gave Jacob Esau's clothes to put on, then covered his arms and neck with goatskin — for Esau was very hirsute. Then she thrust Jacob before his father. Isaac hesitated at first, but the smell of Esau's clothes convinced him. He gave Jacob the blessing that was meant for Esau.

Govert Flinck had been a pupil of Rembrandt's from about 1632 to 1636. In 1636, he established himself as an independent painter in Amsterdam. Rembrandt's influence on Flinck was — as with all his pupils — great: Flinck often chose the same subjects as Rembrandt, and he developed his style on the model of that of his master. He adopted Rembrandt's 'chiaroscuro' effects, but not his favourite colours. Flinck preferred a more violent palette, dark red, reddish brown, very dark green; in this way he made a painting very pleasant to look at. But Rembrandt could not teach his pupil Govert Flinck how to convey the real emotions of his biblical characters.

44. GOVERT FLINCK
Born 25th January 1615 at Cleves
Died 2nd February 1660
at Amsterdam.

ISAAC BLESSING JACOB
Canvas, 117 cm. × 141 cm.
Was signed and dated: 1638;
Amsterdam, Rijksmuseum.

The blessing of Joseph's children by his father Jacob is an often-depicted subject. It is generally used on account of the symbolism of the action: by giving his blessing to Ephraim, the younger son, Jacob is blessing Christendom, of which Ephraim is the symbol.

However, Rembrandt did not, in his painting, follow the traditional representation of the story. Old Jacob, as the Bible relates, wants to give his blessing to the two children of his favourite son Joseph before his death. In accordance with the Jewish tradition, he must give the blessing to Manasseh, the elder son, with his right hand, and to the younger, fair-haired son, Ephraim, with his left. But Jacob blesses Ephraim with his right hand. Joseph mentions his mistake to him and then Jacob says: "I know that, my son, I know that. But Ephraim shall be greater than Manasseh, his descendants shall become the most perfect of races."

In early Christian art, Jacob's action of blessing is always represented with his hands crossed: the elder son stands in front of Jacob on his right, but Jacob is blessing him with his left hand; he is laying his right hand on the head of Ephraim, who is standing in front of him on his left. And Joseph is generally trying, with a gesture, to rectify his father's mistake. But Rembrandt did not bother about tradition. There is no question of a disagreement between father and son: Jacob blesses Ephraim and Joseph indicates his approval of this. Joseph's wife Asnath is never usually present for the blessing: the Bible does not mention her. But Rembrandt could not depict such a solemn occasion without the presence of the mother. He therefore also included Asnath, who is moved, and deep in thought.

Compared with the blessing of Jacob by Isaac which Flinck painted (p. 44), Rembrandt's picture has the very thing that is lacking from Flinck's work: Rembrandt also knew how to make us feel the emotions of his characters; he goes further than to depict purely an event.

45. REMBRANDT VAN RIJN
Born 15th July 1606 at Leiden
Died 4th October 1669 at Amsterdam.

JACOB BLESSING
EPHRAIM AND MANASSEH
"JACOB'S BLESSING"
Canvas, 175.5 cm. × 210.5 cm.
signed and dated: 1656;
Kassel, Staatliche Kunstsammlungen.

Saul, God's anointed king of the Israelites, was an unhappy man. He had been disobedient to God, and now an evil spirit was tormenting him. In order to alleviate his attacks of depression, his servants sought out a cithern-player for him, and so David became Saul's servant. When the Philistines attacked the Israelites again, only David was able to kill their hero Goliath with a sling and a stone. And all the people praised David. But Saul was possessed by a raging hatred against David. He tried twice to kill him with a spear.

Rembrandt's Saul is a pitiful person, despite his regal splendour, his rich velvet cloak, the golden tunic, the crown bound round with a silk turban. The dark attacks of depression have him in their power, but the music of the cithern can move him to tears. The deadly hatred is not yet roused in Saul's heart, but nevertheless Rembrandt gives him the spear, held firmly in his hand, with which he will later try to murder David. When this miscarries, Saul robbed of his reason, will chase David completely throughout his land. But David triumphs. Soon he is the king with the golden crown and the velvet cloak. As yet, however, he sits as a humble servant in a little corner, immersed in his cithern-playing. Saul's loneliness is absolute in Rembrandt's picture: a dark red velvet curtain conceals the pathetic king from his servant. There is no longer any contact possible between the two.

46. REMBRANDT VAN RIJN
Born 15th July 1606 at Leiden
Died 4th October 1669 at Amsterdam.

SAUL AND DAVID
Canvas, 130.5 cm. × 164 cm.
c. 1657;
The Hague, Mauritshuis.

Titus was not a monk. But it is not so surprising that Rembrandt was eager to paint his son in a Capucin's habit. All the shades of brown, of which Rembrandt was so fond, could be found in a habit like that. This kind of habit isolates the face of the subject from the background, so that all the attention can be concentrated on the face alone.

Rembrandt probably did not just want to paint his son in a monk's habit. He needed him as a model — a model for a portrait of St. Francis of Assisi. St. Francis was not a favourite saint with Catholics only, he was also popular with Protestants. They too felt themselves inspired by the events of the life of the man who had been the son of a rich cloth-merchant, but gave up all his possessions and dedicated himself solely to the helping of the sick and the poor from then on. There was an order of Franciscan monks in Holland. The order which St. Francis himself had founded had split up into different orders in later centuries. One of these, the Capucin order, was particularly widespread in Holland; the order was established there in 1585. Despite the fact that the Protestant Church was the official state religion, the order was still able to continue with its work on a limited scale. Rembrandt must therefore have been able to see Capucin monks with his own eyes.

Titus is only nineteen here. His fine, pale face stands out very clearly from the hood of the monk's habit. Occasionally it has been supposed that Saskia suffered from tuberculosis and that it was the cause of her early death, of that of her children, and also that of Titus. Titus only lived to the age of 27; he died seven months after his marriage to Magdalena van Loo. Their little daughter Titia was born six months after Titus' death.

47. REMBRANDT VAN RIJN
Born 15th July 1606 at Leiden
Died 4th October 1669 at Amsterdam.

TITUS VAN RIJN
AS ST. FRANCIS
Canvas, 79.5 cm. × 67.5 cm.
signed and dated: 166(0);
Amsterdam, Rijksmuseum.

Jesus was taken prisoner and brought to the house of the High Priest. Peter followed the group at a distance. In the courtyard a fire was burning, and the soldiers went to sit by it. Peter joined them. But, by the light of the fire, a maid-servant saw him sitting there and said: "this man was also with him". But Peter said: "I do not know him".

And another person also said: "you were with him". Again Peter denied it. An hour later, a third person said: "this man was with him too", and again Peter said vehemently, "I do not know what you are talking about, woman". Then the cock crowed and Jesus, who was standing within before the High Priest, turned round and looked at Peter. He remembered clearly that Jesus had prophesied to him that he would deny Jesus three times before the cock crowed. He went outside and wept bitterly.

Rembrandt chose the third and last denial for his painting: in the background, Jesus is looking round at Peter. But Rembrandt wanted most of all to portray the action between the two main characters: the servant, eager for sensation, who is examining Peter's face even more clearly by the light of a candle, and Peter, who is denying her challenge with an innocent look and a grandiose gesture.

This time the details of the story provide the light. But Rembrandt did not take the great fire mentioned in the Bible as his source of light, but used something more direct: the glimmering of a candle between Peter and the servant-maid. The soldier is only a looker-on. He creates a distance between the viewer and the main characters, although the favourite effects of light are depicted on his armour.

48. REMBRANDT VAN RIJN
Born 15th July 1606 at Leiden
Died 4th October 1669 at Amsterdam.

ST. PETER'S DENIAL
Canvas, 154 cm. × 169 cm.
signed and dated: 1660;
Amsterdam, Rijksmuseum.

Of all the countries which Dutch ships sailed to, Africa was not, comparatively speaking, very far away. There were also Dutch settlements there: the Cape of Good Hope and the Gold Coast. Negroes can hardly have been an unusual sight for seventeenth-century Dutchmen, and certainly not for the inhabitants of the port of Amsterdam. But to pick on them for a portrait was much less usual. However, Rembrandt had really no interest in tradition or the examples of others: he could see clearly with his own eyes how a negro should be depicted, in such a way that he did not look like a blackened white man.

In Rembrandt's inventory of 1656, there was mention of a picture of two moors painted by the master, which was in the large studio on the first floor. Rembrandt had therefore probably painted another portrait of two negroes in the years before this portrait. This picture is, in any case, a painting done in the '60s. Rembrandt was finding it less and less important to depict every detail carefully: a slight indication of gold stripes on a green coat was enough for him. A bright patch of light on the clothing of one negro separates his head from his body; shadow alone is used for the head of the other, leaning heavily on the arm of his companion.

49. REMBRANDT VAN RIJN
Born 15th July 1606 at Leiden
Died 4th October 1669 at Amsterdam.

TWO NEGROES
Canvas, 77.5 cm. × 64.5 cm.
signed and dated: 1661;
The Hague, Mauritshuis.

50. REMBRANDT VAN RIJN
Born 15th July 1606 at Leiden
Died 4th October 1669 at Amsterdam.

SELF-PORTRAIT
AS THE APOSTLE PAUL
Canvas, 91 cm. × 77 cm.
signed and dated: 1661;
Amsterdam, Rijksmuseum.

The apostle Paul is one of the most puzzling characters in the New Testament. He was originally a keen persecutor of the Christians and then a fervant convert to Christ. Divine intervention does indeed seem necessary to bring about such a change in the life of a man. Paul made long missionary journeys, wrote letters incessantly to all the Christian communities, and finally had to pay for his activity with his death: in 64, he was beheaded with a sword in Rome. Since then, the sword has been the attribute of St. Paul. And that is why Rembrandt must have been painting himself as the apostle Paul: in this self-portrait, he has the hilt of a sword protruding from under his coat. Rembrandt painted St. Paul on another occasion, as an old man with a long grey beard, made prisoner by the Romans, but still busy writing letters. Rembrandt also has letters beside him in this self-portrait. They seem to be letters in Hebrew, written on vellum; Rembrandt must not have known that Paul wrote his letters in Greek. But although the reason for Rembrandt's choosing the apostle Paul for a self-portrait is unknown, it is clear that Rembrandt was here again trying, in a different manner from all his other self-portraits, to depict his own ego.

The life of success was over, but even so the committee of the Drapers' Guild ordered their portrait from him, and he was also chosen to work on the decoration of the pride of Amsterdam: the new Town Hall. And what is more: although he had been a practising painter for some forty years, he discovered again and again a new way of creating a masterpiece with canvas and paint.

The Staalmeesters exercised control over the dying of baize. That is a woollen fabric that is now used only for covering billiard-tables, but in the seventeenth century, cities like Leiden, and Amsterdam too, owed a good deal of their prosperity to the baize industry.

In 1661, the 'Staalmeesters' of the time in Amsterdam decided to have their portrait painted, and they chose Rembrandt to paint it. The portrait was to be hung in the 'Staalhof', the building where the Staalmeesters held their meetings; it is still standing in the Staalstraat in Amsterdam. They had also decided on the place for the picture: very high up, perhaps well above a mantelpiece. Rembrandt also had to consider this: the table and the people behind it have the right perspective only when the painting hangs above eye-level. The grouping of five people round a table so that it did not become a stiff representation is a problem that painters before and after Rembrandt have wrestled with. Rembrandt also had to — quite a lot. X-ray photographs of the painting have been taken and they show that Rembrandt later made alterations in the attitude of nearly all the figures. And beforehand, before he began the painting, Rembrandt had made drawings of all the Staalmeesters separately; three of the drawings still exist.

The sixth man in the painting, the one without a hat and wearing a very simple white collar, was the servant of the Staalhof, and had therefore to be satisfied with his modest position.

After a career of almost forty years as a painter, Rembrandt knew that the suggestion of forms and materials is often much more effective than the careful and detailed imitation of them. He therefore just indicated that there was a Persian carpet on the table, but did not even make the pattern recognizable. The painting on the chimney-breast is of a lighthouse. That is the symbol of the quality that the board of Staalmeesters must possess in a great measure: vigilance, attentiveness and trustworthyness.

51. REMBRANDT VAN RIJN
Born 15th July 1606 at Leiden
Died 4th October 1669 at Amsterdam.

"THE STAALMEESTERS"
THE SAMPLING-OFFICIALS
OF THE CLOTH-MAKERS'
GUILD AT AMSTERDAM
Canvas, 191.5 cm. × 279 cm.
signed and dated: 1662 (?);
Amsterdam, Rijksmuseum.

Years before Rembrandt was given the commission to do the painting of the Staalmeesters (pl. 51), his former pupil, Ferdinand Bol, had been engaged in a similar commission: a portrait of the four governors of the Lepers' Hospital. At the time, in 1649, Bol was a painter of some fifteen years' independence. He had developed the style of painting he had learnt from Rembrandt to as smooth, elegant way of painting. He made a flattering portrait of his sitters, and he devoted a great deal of attention to everything else that had to be included in a picture.

The Lepers' Home was the building where people who suffered from lepra (= leprosy) chose to be sequestered apart from the community. It was thought then that leprosy was very contagious, which is why lepers were kept shut well away from the community. When in the streets, they often had rattles with them, in order to warn people that they were approaching. Naturally, all kinds of people did come into Lepers' Homes who were not suffering from leprosy, but from other diseases. The little boy in Bol's painting, who has been brought in by the house-father, the head of the Home, is not suffering from leprosy, but has another illness which makes the skin on the head inflamed: 'tinea capitis' (scaldhead).

A proven way of bringing some life into a group of sombre, black-clad men like this one, is to make one of the principal figures stand. Often, too, one of these brightly-coloured Persian carpets was laid on the table; Dutch people practically never used them as floor-coverings, but much more often as table-covers. Rembrandt also did that with his 'Staalmeesters', though that work was rather more refined than Bol's of the year 1649.

52. FERDINAND BOL
Baptised 24th June 1616 at Dordrecht
Buried 24th July 1680 at Amsterdam.

THE GOVERNORS
OF THE LEPERS' HOSPITAL
IN AMSTERDAM
Canvas, 224 cm. × 310 cm.
signed and dated: 1649;
Amsterdam, Rijksmuseum.

When the merchant Frederik Rihel died in Amsterdam in 1681, he left no will. The personal effects in his house on the Herengracht were therefore sealed until an inventory of them was made shortly afterwards. Rihel possessed a lot of silver, porcelain, paintings. One of the paintings was "the likeness of the deceased on horseback by Rembrandt". Now it very rarely happened in Holland that anyone had his portrait painted as a rider on a horse. But Frederik Riher was of an international disposition. He originated from Strasbourg and his bags of merchandise and money travelled all over the world. From the inventory, with its numerous handsome suits of clothes, many of them embellished with lace, or fringes or brightly-coloured sashes, it seems clear that Rihel was a man concerned with outward show. For him, a portrait on horseback was the obvious kind, for he was mad about horses: when he could only just get by, he had his own horses, and then he also demanded of his succession of servants that they must be accustomed to horses. On his death in 1681, he possessed "two dapple-grey horses" in a stable on the Reguliersmarkt, plus a coach and an open carriage.

In 1660, the ten-year-old Willem III made a state visit to Amsterdam. One hundred and eight horsemen from Amsterdam also rode in the royal procession, in three groups; between the second and the third groups came the coach containing the prince. Frederik Rihel was a member of the third group and rode close behind the coach with the prince in. It was on the occasion in question that Frederik Rihel had his portrait on horseback painted by Rembrandt. That is why Rembrandt clearly painted the coach in the background, with the profile of the young prince in a patch of light.

Rembrandt's portrait of Frederik Rihel is life-size: after "The Night Watch", it is his largest painting. It is a fitting portrait for a man who lived in almost un-Dutch high state. He must have had a good place for it in the huge (rented) houses which he occupied in turn. Actually, the equestrian portrait was not the only one of himself that he possessed: "a likeness of the same on foot" and "a likeness of the deceased in a carved gilded frame" also appear in Rihel's inventory of 1661, made after his death.

53. REMBRANDT VAN RIJN
Born 15th July 1606 at Leiden
Died 4th October 1669 at Amsterdam.

FREDERIK RIHEL (C. 1626 – 1681)
ON HORSEBACK
Canvas, 282 cm. × 248 cm.
signed and dated: 166(3);
London, National Gallery.

In the summer of 69 A. D., Julius — also known as Claudius — Civilis decided to free his people, the Batavians, from Roman domination. Under the pretext of a sacrificial celebration, he called the leaders of the people together in a sacred wood. There he represented the disadvantages of being subject so movingly that they all, as one man, swore an oath against the Romans. That was the beginning of the uprising of the Batavians, which proceeded with much success at first, but finally failed in 70. The Netherlanders of 1660 saw in the Batavians' oath a parallel with their war against the Spaniards, which ended with the Peace of Münster in 1648.

When the Town Hall of Amsterdam (now the Palace) in the Dam was to be decorated, the theme chosen for the decoration of the central gallery was also episodes from the Batavians' uprising. The commission for this was given to Govert Flinck, but when he had just begun to plan the series on a large scale, he died. Then the commission was divided up between several different painters. Rembrandt's commission was for "The Oath of the Batavians". The canvas was to be five and a half metres square, and was destined for the south-east corner of the gallery.

In 1662, a certain Melchior Fokkens wrote a book about Amsterdam, in which there also appears a description of the decorations of the Town Hall. He mentions a picture of the oath of the Batavians, painted by Rembrandt, in the south-east corner of the great gallery.

But in 1663, a painting by the artist Jurriaen Ovens, also of the oath of the Batavians, was put in that place. Either Rembrandt's painting was moved immediately after it was put in position, therefore, or Melchior Fokkens anticipated events, and Rembrandt's "Oath" never did actually hang there.

In 1891, it was discovered that a painting in the museum at Stockholm which was known as "The Covenant of the Bohemian captain Ziska" was the middle piece of Rembrandt's "Oath of Covenant of the Batavians". Only a quarter of the original composition is left and it is not known what happened to the rest. We know Rembrandt's original composition only from a quickly-sketched drawing: six steps lead up to a big vaulted room, in which Julius Civilis sits at an enormous table with a large group of Batavians.

54. REMBRANDT VAN RIJN
Born 15th July 1606 at Leiden
Died 4th October 1669 at Amsterdam.

THE OATH OF COVENANT
OF THE BATAVIANS
UNDER JULIUS CIVILIS
"THE CONSPIRACY
OF CLAUDIUS CIVILIS"
Canvas, 196 cm. × 309 cm.
Painted in 1661/1662;
Stockholm, National Museum.

Family-portraits were not unusual in seventeenth-century Dutch art. The Dutch painters really did have a preference for the intimate, and sometimes for cosiness. And there is nothing more intimate than a father and mother with their children beside them, often even depicted in the setting of their own home. Now the biggest problem in the painting of a group-portrait of this kind was the creation of unity, really depicting the people as a group. That could be achieved by the composition, but also by having the subjects touching each other, looking at each other, having children play with something, or having one of them hand something to another: a flower, an apple. Rembrandt naturally knew all these often-used methods too: he even uses them in this family-portrait. But yet Rembrandt made of this scene a portrait such as had never before been painted of a couple. For, apart from the actual gestures which provide contact, he brought to his painting a spiritual contact which goes far beyond gestures.

Rembrandt did not need to use a congenial Dutch interior in creating intimacy: it can hardly be seen where the family is.

In the last years of his life, Rembrandt no longer "finished off" his paintings. When, at the end of 1688, Cosimo de' Medici visited Rembrandt's studio together with the printer Pieter Blaeu, they found, to their astonishment, no 'completely finished' painting. But the ideas of visitors and host concerning what was a really finished painting must indeed have been rather different. Rembrandt no longer had need of definite forms to make an idea, an emotion very concrete.

55. REMBRANDT VAN RIJN
Born 15th July 1606 at Leiden
Died 4th October 1669 at Amsterdam.

PORTRAIT OF A FAMILY
WITH THREE CHILDREN
"THE FAMILY GROUP"
Canvas, 126 cm. × 167 cm.
signed, c. 1668;
Brunswick,
Herzog Anton Ulrich Museum.

At the beginning of the nineteenth century, someone saw in this painting the picture of a Jewish father hanging a chain round the neck of his daughter on the occasion of her wedding. Since then, the picture has been called "The Jewish Bride". But the title cannot be the correct one at all. It is impossible to say with certainty that the girl is Jewish; whether she really is a bride is not at all clear, as nothing indicates whether she is or not. The man is generally no longer seen as someone of an older generation, but as her partner. But this is not a normal portrait of a couple. The unusually rich red and gold costumes do point towards a definite event. Almost all the Old Testament couples have been suggested by writers, but never completely to the satisfaction of everyone. A good many names of couples of Rembrandt's time have also been put forward, without any one couple ever really seeming to be the right one. The picture must thus remain anonymous for the time being. The painting itself tells us nothing either for or against any suggestion. Rembrandt painted a masterpiece of love between two people: she is shy and modest, he is authoritative, protective.

Rembrandt used glowing colours; the paint itself gives body to the material of the costumes: he added definite patterns to the material with his palette-knife and the other end of his brush.

For Rembrandt, hands were often the 'instruments' with which human emotions could be made tangible: in blessing, in embracing. Thus he here makes hands interpret emotions, without exaggeration, without any dramatic scene.

56. REMBRANDT VAN RIJN
Born 15th July 1606 at Leiden
Died 4th October 1669 at Amsterdam.

"THE JEWISH BRIDE"
Canvas. 121.5 cm. × 166.5 cm.
signed, c. 1665;
Amsterdam, Rijksmuseum.

Ernst van Beveren, the lord of West-IJsselmonde and De Linde was progressing on an important political career: first he was sheriff of Dordrecht, then Lord Mayor and, in 1704, postmaster. In the seventeenth century, Dordrecht was a very large town, and not unimportant as a centre of trade. To what extent Van Beveren really carried out his political functions with due zeal is not known. It happened often enough that the lords got the titles and the money and their servants had to do the work for a small part of the salary.

Ernst van Beveren is only twenty-five years old in De Gelder's painting. He does not look like just anyone: he is depicted with a lot of splendour and show. During his training as a painter, Aert de Gelder must have been taught by master Rembrandt to dress people in gay and fantastic costumes: Rembrandt himself was very keen on doing that too. That is why Van Beveren is wearing a splendid gold-bordered cloak over a green and gold suit. Definitely not the dress the sheriffs of Dordrecht wore every day! Above all the splendour, Van Beveren has a rather impressive, somewhat reserved face. De Gelder had him make a rhetorical gesture: his right hand is thrust out before him. This was definitely also a means for the artist to let people see a little sample of his ability. Aert de Gelder very often used a trick of perspective like this one.

Aert de Gelder was the one who, of all Rembrandt's pupils, remained faithful to his master's style, even long after he had ceased to be Rembrandt's pupil.

57. AERT DE GELDER
Born 1645 at Dordrecht
Died 1727 at Dordrecht.

ERNST VAN BEVEREN (1660-1722)
Canvas, 128 cm. × 105 cm.
signed and dated: 1685;
Amsterdam, Rijksmuseum.

By using parables, Jesus tried to make his disciples clearly aware of what was essential to the belief in God. One of the most fascinating of the parables is the story of the prodigal son. The son has squandered away his part of his inheritance from his father on drink and women. In great poverty, he finally has to look after swine. After hesitating for a long time, he then decides to go back to this father's house. The father is still looking out for his son. Full of gladness, he clasps the son who has returned in his arms. His other son, who has always loyally helped his father, looks on jealously. It was the feelings that were beyond everyday human experience in many biblical stories that struck Rembrandt. The deep humility of the son, the pity of the father — Rembrandt could depict such emotions more and more powerfully with less and less means. The figures in this painting are almost life-size. Without attempting to arrange a dramatic pose, Rembrandt depicts the father and son from the front. The warm red garment of the father gives extra emphasis to the sign of blessing in which he has placed both hands on the back of his son.

The attendant figures were probably painted by a pupil; they have no other function in the picture. The son in the background is taken from the text in the Bible, which tells that the second son was also present at the reception of the prodigal son.

58. REMBRANDT VAN RIJN
Born 15th July 1606 at Leiden
Died 4th October 1669 at Amsterdam.

THE RETURN OF THE
PRODIGAL SON
Canvas, 262 cm. × 206 cm.
signed, c. 1664;
Leningrad, Hermitage.

Gerbrand van den Eeckhout was, as was Roelant Roghman, one of Rembrandt's most faithful friends. In the years 1635—1640, he had been Rembrandt's pupil and he was still practising his master's style long afterwards, above all in his religious paintings. In his portraits and genre-pictures, he did not imitate Rembrandt's example so much.

The choice of biblical stories made by Van den Eeckhout for his paintings was often parallelled by what Rembrandt depicted from the Bible in his drawings, etchings and paintings. The story of St. Peter healing the paralytic was also once illustrated by Rembrandt. When the apostles Peter and John were going into the temple one day, they came upon a man with paralysis by the entrance, who had been brought there and set down so that he could beg. He also asked Peter and John for alms. "Gold and silver have I not," said Peter, "but what I have I give to you: in the name of Jesus, walk!" And the man stood up and ran rejoicing into the temple.

However much Van den Eeckhout was dependent on what he learnt from Rembrandt, he was nevertheless unable to put any real tension into his pictures. He used eloquent gestures, but they remain gestures, they do not convey the essence of the story.

Van den Eeckhout followed tradition in depicting the apostles: St. Peter is old, with a short white beard, St. John is a young man.

The woman with the two children who give such a lively effect, is wearing the big flat hat which was for a very long time regarded in representational art as being typical for a Jewish woman.

59. GERBRAND VAN DEN EECKHOUT
Born 9th August 1621 at Amsterdam
Buried 29th September 1674
at Amsterdam.

SAINT PETER HEALING THE LAME
Canvas, 61 cm. × 69.5 cm.
signed and dated: 1667;
San Francisco,
The Young Memorial Museum.

Although this self-portrait is often described as the picture of a man on the threshold of death, Rembrandt certainly did not know when he painted this self-portrait that he would die that year.

On the 8th October 1669, the verger of the Westerkerk wrote in the book of burials that he had that day buried in the church, Rembrandt van Rijn, a painter from the Rozengracht.

Rembrandt had worked as a painter for a good forty years. Some 400 paintings, 300 etchings and 200 drawings still bear witness to an active life: originally there would certainly have been more. It is known of about thirty-five painters who were pupils of Rembrandt.

In 1660, Rembrandt had had to exchange his large, spacious house in Sint Anthoniesbreestraat for a much smaller dwelling on the Rozengracht, in that part of the city which was later known as "the Jordan". The district was laid out only after 1662, with the intention of settling small industries there, such as tanneries, silk-weavers and -dyers, pinmakers, etc. But the neighbourhood was also occupied by the people who worked in the little industries. There were very small houses, really too small to have a studio, run an art-dealer's and still have living-space for a familiy of four persons: Rembrandt, Hendrickje, their little daughter Cornelia and Titus. But in 1669, Rembrandt and Cornelia were left alone; Hendrickje had died in 1662 and Titus had followed her in 1668.

Rembrandt would then be round about 63 years old, and although he had had to take many blows from life, this portrait is painted just as surely and powerfully as his portraits of the '50s. He only made a small change later: he covered the white beret with goldcoloured stripes, so that it harmonized better with the finely-painted background, the greying hair and the pink tones of the face.

By the time he died, the genial painter Rembrandt had really lived too long. Public taste preferred smoother, lighter paintings. For the time being, quality could not triumph over the reigning fashion.

60. REMBRANDT VAN RIJN
Born 15th July 1606 at Leiden
Died 4th October 1669 at Amsterdam.

SELF-PORTRAIT
Canvas, 59 cm. × 61 cm.
signed and dated: 1669;
The Hague, Mauritshuis.